# A Love That Dares to Question

## to Question

*A bishop challenges his church*

## Bishop John Heaps

CANTERBURY
PRESS

Norwich

© John Heaps 2001

First UK edition published in 2001 by The Canterbury
Press Norwich (a publishing imprint of Hymns Ancient
& Modern Limited, a registered charity)
St Mary's Works, St Mary's Plain,
Norwich, Norfolk, NR3 3BH

First published in 1998 by Aurora Books, Australia

British Library Cataloguing in Publication Data

A catalogue record for this book is available
from the British Library

ISBN 1-85311-398-0

Printed in Great Britain by
Biddles Ltd, *www.biddles.co.uk*

*Love . . .*
*is*
*always ready*
*to*
*excuse*
*to*
*trust*
*to*
*hope*
(1 Cor. 15: 6–7)

# CONTENTS

# 1. LET LOVE LOOSE IN THE WORLD

The Jubilee Year, we all know, was not essentially about pilgrimages, indulgences for visiting churches and praying there, special commemorative medals or stamps or even special religious events. It was about forgiveness and about wiping out debts. The Pope has shown himself to be a world leader in many ways. He has also spoken of the power of example and life as teachers.

There are many people estranged from the Church who love God and his people and serve God and neighbour as best they can. All they need is a word of forgiveness and a sign to welcome them home.

"Offer forgiveness and receive peace" was the heading of Pope John Paul II's 1997 New Year Message. What a wonderful sign it would be to the world if the Pope were to lead the way, not only as he so lovingly did by forgiving the man who attempted to kill him, but by tearing down the walls which block the way to reconciliation to thousands.

"With deep conviction I wish to appeal to everyone to seek peace along the path of forgiveness. I am fully aware that forgiveness can seem contrary to human logic, which often yields to the dynamics of conflict and revenge. But forgiveness is inspired by the logic of love." This theme and these words are set in the context of: "Only three years separate us from the dawn of the new millennium."

There are those good priests who have found that celibacy is not their vocation. Many would rejoice at a word of gratitude for what they have done and given, and a word of welcome back to the priestly ministry or back to full union with the Church without reservations or restrictions.

There are those good people who live in long-lasting, life-giving relationships, who are told by Church officials to go back to a former relationship which proved to be destructive and untrue, or to walk away from spouse and family, or to live a celibate life together. These solutions range from the impossible to the sinful. These good people need a word of reconciliation and welcome.

Others find that the requirement of integral confession is a stumbling block. Yet where there are repentance, reparation for damage done, and love, it seems contradictory that the Church's own law should stand in the way of reconciliation. The reconciling words of Jesus were simple. He knew that love of God and sin could not co-exist in one heart.

Then there are those theologians who have honestly sought a better way of expressing the eternal truths and a way to live the Christian life with authenticity and compassion, who need a generous attitude of open listening and a warm welcome into the heart of a loving Church.

All could be done generously and graciously, ushering in a new attitude of deeper and more complete trust

Have you ever received a favour, yet felt it was given grudgingly? There are those double messages like, "You may go if you like, but think of me here at home all alone." Such "favours" certainly do not fill people with a spirit of freedom and joy as they go on their way.

In a conversation with an old friend not long ago, an aside revealed something lingering in his memory that I had not realized before. At the time of his wedding he was not a Catholic, his wife was. They were married in the sacristy of the church, out of view of their families and friends. There was still a sadness in his voice as he said, "My family and guests wondered where we had got to *It seems contradictory that the Church's own law should stand in the way of reconciliation.* for such a long time. Then we came back and went down the aisle as husband and wife." His day of joy had been clouded and the cloud had never fully lifted.

This situation would never occur today and I suppose most of us wonder how anyone ever thought it up. It was supposed to discourage mixed marriages. I don't know what it was supposed to say about human relationships and genuine love in selecting a partner for life.

A dispensation, given with the condition that the marriage would not take place before the altar in the church, is the type of ungracious giving to which I refer. Surely if we offer forgiveness, a dispensation or any favour, it should be done with wholehearted graciousness and joy at being able to welcome the happiness of others.

The sad situation is that in other areas the same attitude of ungracious giving still persists. An obvious example is the way a priest is treated when he comes to the painful but honest conclusion that he is unable to continue in the ministry under the conditions required by Rome. Neither the manner of obtaining a dispensation nor the conditions under which it is given exude graciousness and generosity.

Generosity, courtesy, sensitivity and pastoral care are all aspects of the one commandment given by Jesus to form and regulate all our relationships with each other. Genuine love will never, and can never, undermine the Church or encourage "easy and hollow solutions", for God is love.

I attempt to develop some of these ideas and look at some other issues of pastoral care and justice in these few pages. Nothing will change for the better if it is not based on, and coming from, a deep spiritual foundation.

As the Church takes full advantage of responding

to the Year of Jubilee, it will speak with an authentic and more audible voice in calling others to respond to the "logic of love" if this is truly its own logic. It is an opportunity not only to wipe out debts, but to begin to live in a different way. As we attempt to do this ourselves, we can ask nations to work, not from suspicion and hatred but from trust and love, to show some signs that trust is possible and that it has positive results. We can call on those with the power to liberate poor countries crushed under massive foreign debts to be liberators and gracious givers. Just as in the case of a generous Church, the nations will receive much more than they give. None will lose when love is let loose in the world.

# 2. THE GOOD NEWS IS A HUMAN BEING

We are asked to read the signs of the times and to respond.

If reading the signs of the times seems too abstract a request, read *The Times* or the *Independent*, or whatever the local newspaper is called. Then read why Jesus was sent. These are the words of Isaiah, the prophet, which Jesus made his own: "The spirit of the Lord has been given to me, for he has anointed me. He has sent me to bring good news to the poor, to proclaim liberty to captives and to the blind new sight, to set the downtrodden free, to proclaim the Lord's year of favour" (Lk. 4:18-19). This is not about another world or another time, it is supposed to be happening now. Christ, the anointed of God, is supposed to be making a difference to the lives of the poor and the rejected. His chosen way of doing this is through his followers. We are commissioned to bring this good news to the nations. We can do this only by

6

being one spirit with Jesus. Living his life, we will be authentic teachers, as he was.

There is no such thing as uninvolved, private holiness for its own sake. The message of Jesus is not given to us to hide under a tub, or to keep us happy and safe and separated from others.

God chose to bring human beings into life and happiness through other human beings. God chose that a human being would be the way to God. His Word became flesh to dwell among us and his Word spoke to us, healed us and redeemed us in human flesh. This was God's chosen way and it is still God's chosen way. He still chooses to speak to us, heal us, lift us up and reconcile us through human beings. The good news is a human being. The good news must still be lived in and spoken through human beings.

*We must surely ask: "What has gone wrong? In what ways is the Church defective? How are we failing in our call to be and to bring good news?"*

When we compare the good news with the world news, we can't help concluding that something has gone wrong. I am sure that no matter how perfect the Church was or how holy the followers of Christ were, we would still have the destructive evils of selfishness, greed, and obstinacy. No matter how much evil there is in the world, we still have the inspiring beauty of lives lived in unselfish and generous love. Having said this, I am still uncomfortable with the inconsistencies when I read something like: "In him a new age has dawned, the long reign of sin is ended, a broken world has been renewed, and man is once again made whole" (Preface of Easter IV), or "As King he claims dominion over all creation, that he may present to you, his almighty Father, an eternal and universal kingdom: a kingdom of truth and life, a kingdom of holiness and grace, a kingdom of justice, love and peace" (Preface of Christ the King).

My consolation comes from the faithful people who are constantly striving to bring about this blessed state. My sadness comes from the apparent shallowness of faith in the lives of those who have not only allowed cruel injustices to flourish, but have been part of the process and structure of injustice. My object is not to judge anyone. To judge anyone as a sinner is beyond our capacity. It is an irrational act itself. It is possible, however, to look at the activity and inactivity of Christians and so-called Christian nations and to conclude that the outcome of their actions and inaction is not a reflection of the kingdom referred to above. If we care we must surely ask, "What has gone wrong? In what ways is the Church defective? How are we failing in our call to be and to bring good news?"

Jesus gave us just two commandments. Everything else is contained in these. If we keep them we will not break any of the ten commandments, we will live by the beatitudes and be one with God and one with his children. These commandments are, of course, to love God totally and to love our neighbour as ourselves. Has this been the centre of the life of my Church and of my personal and communal life?

As a young man, I, like other Catholics of my time, was very conscious of my duty to God and to the Church, to pray for the salvation of souls and of my own desire to save my soul. We were given details of how these things might be accomplished. We were to do certain things and to avoid certain actions. In some cases the rules were spelt out in fine detail. If we transgressed by failing to perform our duties or by doing those proscribed things, our relationship with God was either weakened or lost altogether. All could be restored by a good confession. Here again, there were exact rules on which the outcome depended. Even if love of God was not the motive for sorrow, fear of the loss of God for eternity was sufficient, with absolution.

Fear was used as a motivating force to keep us close to God. Those of us who lived through those times can probably recall some powerful mission sermons. I still remember one on hell. The preacher spoke of the torments of the damned. Then he spoke of eternity in this wretched condition. He asked us to imagine a steel ball as big as the Earth, then a little bird brushing this huge ball with its wing once every thousand years. If ever the little bird wore the steel ball away, the time it took would have made no impression on eternity. People flocked to confession. The mission was acclaimed a great success.

This look back into the past is not for the purpose of colour, or to criticize dedicated and fervent people. I have mentioned it to help us understand what has happened since those times. Present day preachers are sometimes criticized for talking of nothing but love and its implications. People will ask what has happened to sin and to hell. The first point I wish to make is that the only relationship that will make us happy with God in eternity is love. We cannot be with God in a state of fear. We could not possibly enjoy the presence of the all-loving Father while we hate any one of his children.

People have left the Church or ceased active contact with the Church for all sorts of reasons. Acknowledging this, the second point is to observe what happened when the emphasis on sin and hell was lessened. People left us in droves. This causes me to ask: what sort of a Church did we have when the motive for worship or for morality was fear? How does it all fit in with a relationship of love of God, a desire to be one with Christ, a longing for his Kingdom of justice, love and peace to come? Without judging anyone, would you, on this evidence, say that the strong pre-Vatican Council Church was really the liberating force that Jesus spoke of in his quotation from Isaiah?

Is it unfair to ask how faithful we have been in passing on the beautiful message of Christ?

# 3. RELIGION: A FORCE FOR EVIL

Among the forces that motivate collective action are religion, politics and culture. These are the sources of beliefs, aims, customs and accepted modes of response and reaction to human feelings and life situations. They are also forces which define a community and are points of difference and separation from those outside the group.

If we put a mirror to our times and also look back on history, we may be convinced that the most powerful force of the three is culture. Even where religion is given as the source of division and strife, or as the binding force of the oppressed or the oppressor, I believe the real force is political or cultural. Religion and culture are intertwined, supporting and reinforcing each other. In the purest expression of religion and the noblest culture, this would be a perfect situation. Our mirror to reality gives back a reflection that is far less than noble.

In the reflection, we see: children without limbs, bones visible beneath their skin, more refugees than the world has ever known in its history, millions of hours of work and billions of pounds spent on weapons of mass destruction and personal maiming, killing, revenge, wars, disputes and hatred passed on from generation to generation, an apparent unwillingness to attempt to negotiate and an absence of any trust whatsoever. Much of this is politically motivated and a few are making immense profit from the sufferings of many, but much also has its deep roots in the very religion-culture force I have referred to above.

A letter written to a newspaper recently referred to religion as one of the great forces of evil in the world. I found myself agreeing with the writer. Throughout history and at present, religion is one of the great forces dividing people and preventing or inhibiting reasonable communication and dialogue leading to co-operation and the solution of problems. We don't have to look long or think deeply to find examples.

One night I was listening to a radio programme in which members of the great world religions read from the teachings of their founders. Every one of the readings was inspiring, conducive to a better life, calling for love, understanding and peace.

The difference between what was read and the attitude, interpretation and practice of the followers of the founders was profound. What had happened was that which Jesus had often warned his followers to avoid: turning his teachings into a religion like that practiced by the scribes, Pharisees and lawyers.

When he commanded his followers to go out to all nations, he was telling them to take his life and light to the cultures of the world. His teaching was not to become a cult or a substitute culture or a reason to be a separated, chosen people apart from the world-place in which they lived. They were to go to what was there to inform it, purify it from within and lift it to full human dignity and to present it to God, the Father of all peoples and cultures. "I have come so that they may have life and have it to the full" (Jn.10:10), he had proclaimed, and "You will learn the truth and the truth will make you free" (Jn. 8:32).

When religion becomes an end in itself, gathering political power so as to have its own way, it becomes a force not for full life and freedom, but for the enslaving of minds and even bodies. State religions which favour their adherents in the community and discriminate against outsiders are not the legitimate instruments of God. The minority groups thus inhibited in their freedom can also be reinforced in their own separateness. This very separateness can become a focus of power. As both parties draw their strength and their support from their religion, adherence to the group grows stronger and separation and differences are more clearly defined. Neither the condition of the majority group nor that of the minority has any necessary connection with the Spirit of God.

People have said sometimes that we need a persecution or some outside evil force to bring us back to God and to bind us together into a strong Church again. They observe that the faith flourishes under persecution. I don't believe that persecution is conducive to the growth of anything except the power and wealth of the persecutor. It is true that some may discover a strength that they never before realized they had, but God's gifts through Jesus are freedom and truth. This is the atmosphere in which the true faith and its consequent outcome of justice and love will flourish. Persecution may bring minorities together. If religion is the common bond strengthened by persecution, then it will be all the more reinforced and highlighted. There is nothing like a common enemy to force people into common action. This does not necessarily do anything for the faith. It may do a lot for confirming common practices which are peculiar to the suppressed group. I have observed that when the enemy is no longer the enemy and the cause for solidarity has gone, the fervour of the persecuted begins to be directed into other channels.

From this observation I ask the questions: What was the end result of commitment to the Church in any time of persecution in any country? What was achieved in calling its members together? When the under-privileged, the poor or the downtrodden are us, is there any particular virtue required for standing up for our rights? When we move from being the downtrodden to being the established people, does our sense of social justice evaporate? If religion is merely part of the sub-culture of the minority or if it is merely an element in the culture of the majority, it will be less than the Spirit willed to us by Jesus.

Our culture is part of us. It is something we

have subtly, unconsciously, learned from being born into an existing set of presumptions. Different peoples react to the same human life circumstances and conditions in different ways. No one way is necessarily better than another, it is merely the way we learned to react to the positive and happy things of life and the negative and sad things. A policy of assimilation in a multi-cultural country is not only wrong, but inhumane and irrational. It cannot happen.

Culture, then, is an extremely strong force. The teachings of Jesus and the gift of his Spirit are not given to change cultures, but to take them into the kingdom by the illuminating, liberating power of the Gospel. Thus destructive elements will be

*When religion becomes an end in itself, ... it becomes a force not for full life and freedom, but for the enslaving of minds and even bodies.*

seen as destructive, and creative elements as life-giving. The Spirit of Jesus is not the instrument of any culture or nation or philosophy. All of these are meant to be the instruments of the Gospel.

In bringing the Gospel to the nations and to our nation, we need to go much deeper than catechetics or ritual, to tap the Spirit of Jesus and to prepare the way for true faith. When we observe world events, we must wonder how deeply we have really gone. Jesus told us how to distinguish the real thing from a substitute when he said, "You will be able to tell them by their fruits" (Mt. 7:16). Some of the people most dedicated to religion have perpetrated the most destructive and cruel crimes, even in the name of religion. Again, we ask if there is a better way of being that Church which Jesus sent into the world to be the teacher of all nations.

Having reflected on this question, it would be a mistake to conclude that Jesus came merely to give us a moral code or to establish an organization to call the world to order.

The Gospels are about relationships. Jesus speaks of his relationship with the Father and experiences a deep relationship with the Holy Spirit. It is through our relationship with Jesus that our being is united with absolute love. The disciples who were sent out to all nations had first entered into an intimate relationship with God through Jesus and had experienced the indwelling of the Holy Spirit. It is what Jesus *is* prior to what he *does* that has made the difference in our relationship with God. It is firstly what we are that will make the difference. It is being prior to doing. This fundamental relationship with God will make the difference to all other relationships and choices.

For this reason the basic call of the disciples of Jesus in every age is a call to holiness. We are called to deepen our relationship with God—to allow God to deepen his relationship with us. This spiritual journey will take us to the end of our time and to wherever we are called. Holy people are never complacent, but never over-anxious either. They allow God to work with and through them.

Structures and laws in the Church have as their aim the holiness of God's people. For this reason I have written in subsequent chapters about alternative structures. We need a truly Gospel-centred spirituality. We need to come close to the Divine Word in all the ways he is available to us.

# 4. WHEN LAW IS BAD

The world that Jesus entered was a world where religion was nationalistic, cultic and ritualistic. Each nation had its own gods, its cults and its rituals. All of these supported the nation. For his own people, God was the founder of the nation, its lawgiver and its ruler and protector. In every case, external worship and observance were signs of loyalty, and a lack of observance or an allegiance to another god was interpreted as treason. Jesus called us beyond this and into a deeper relationship with God and with others inside and outside boundaries made by human beings.

His own people believed that they were a nation called into existence by God, a nation whose laws were from God and whose king and protector was God. When things went wrong, they concluded that they had been disobedient to God; when they prospered they were receiving God's reward or forgiveness. There were rituals for the common things of life: for birth, maturity, gratitude for harvests, repentance for sins, for remembering the liberation of their people, and praise and worship of God. There was no such thing as the law of the land as separate from the law of God. The law of the land came from God, so to break the law was to disobey God. Thus a thriving law industry existed and schools of thought and interpretation of the law were an integral part of society. Structures were designed in detail to give expression to the law, and ritual was scrupulously observed and required to be observed by those in authority. They were the chosen people; all others were the rest, the nations, the gentiles.

*For Jesus, nothing came before God, but people came before ritual or rules.*

The immediate followers of Jesus not only encountered the difficulty of dealing with a tightly constructed theocracy at home, but also with the chosen people of Rome and the other cultures to which they came with the Gospel of universal love. To deny the religion or to refuse to enter into the ritual was treason. By contrast to the Jewish people, the pagan religions made no connection between moral conduct and religious performance. One worshipped the gods as a matter of loyalty and as an assurance of success in battle and as a safeguard to the state. It would not be inconsistent behaviour to come from offering incense to a god to giving a thrashing to a slave. Morals were something to do with philosophy and civil life.

In a sense Jesus often spoke and acted against religion. He broke the nationalistic, ritualistic and cultic taboos. He made a deep connection between ritual activity and moral responsibility when he said, "So then, if you are bringing your offering to the altar and there remember that your brother has something against you, leave your offering there before the altar, go and be reconciled with your brother first, and then come back and present your offering" (Mt. 5:23-25). For Jesus, nothing came before God, but people came before ritual or rules. "The Sabbath was made for man not man for the Sabbath" (Mk. 2:27) was his reply to those who criticized his followers for a ritual breaking of the Sabbath interpreted in a very legalistic way. Ritual and law do not exist for their own sake. They are expressions of human needs and the human condition and reality. The means subvert the end by becoming an end. The relative is absolutized—that is, we make idols. Jesus could eat with "sinners" and tax collectors, touch lepers, talk with a Samaritan woman or a Roman soldier. All law should be for freedom.

If law is not conducive to fuller life and liberty, it is bad law. Thus a wise, inner-directed person needs no threat of law. It is safe to say to such a person, "Love, and do as you will." Love will be the motive for activity and for refraining from action. A wise pursuit of the facts and of knowledge will determine the action to be taken, the word to be spoken, or the advice to be offered. At times, silent listening will be the most loving response. A community of mature people should need no more than guidelines agreed upon for the sake of the free-flowing life of people interacting with each other. For example, the community would agree on times of activities together, times and places for meeting or for being silent or alone, and the mode of seeing that services necessary for the life of the community would function smoothly.

Ritual is an important element of life. We should be free to express, in an appropriate way, the thoughts and emotions, beliefs and feelings that are inside us. The constant suppression of feelings is unhealthy for the individual. Suppressed feelings will often be expressed in an inappropriate way, at the wrong time and to the wrong person. Needs, feelings and beliefs belong to groups as well as to individuals.

A true relationship of love needs outward expression. The person who really loves does not need to be told to express that love in some exterior way. It just happens. The person and the community with real love for God do not need to be told to express that love. Love in the heart is expressed in life, is shared with others and acted out in ritual. Such worship will be worship in spirit and in truth.

Thus Jesus gave us a ritual way of remembering him with love and gratitude. This act of remembering, endowed with his power, brings about his actual presence to be the constant source of our life in him. He longed for our worship to be worship in spirit and in truth. To perform a ritual which not only implies but actually prays that we "become one body, one spirit in Christ" (Third Eucharistic Prayer), without longing for and striving for this blessing, is certainly less than worship in spirit and in truth.

What do we need to take us further into the spirit of Christ so that living the Christian life is not merely doing things and avoiding things and keeping to oneself, but is the outward expression of a deep love for God and a love for all God has made?

# 5. Prophets Here and Now

The Gospel accounts of the trial, condemnation, suffering and death of Jesus, and of the response and reaction of all involved, are themselves a mirror to our times and to history. In the whole sad event very few accepted any blame or guilt. Terrible, obviously unjust things were taking place, yet only a few saw that there was any sin or guilt involved. The leaders of the people were acting from religious motives, Pilate was keeping the political balance for the sake of maintaining order, the crowds were following their legitimate leaders, the soldiers were obeying orders, and apparently there were many who did not want to get involved.

This list of motives for action and inaction is repeated over and over throughout history. Christ continues to be crucified in those who suffer from the injustice of powerful people with the co-operation of weak and unthinking people.

It is not until after the event and its outcome

that the crowd realizes the whole thing has been a mistake and a terrible injustice. This happened after the death of Jesus: "When the centurion saw what had taken place, he gave praise to God and said, 'This was a great and good man.' And when all the people who had gathered for the spectacle saw what had happened, they went home beating their breasts" (Lk. 23:47-8).

Seeing the injustice after the event or in the light of history does nothing for those who are the victims of those acts of injustice. Obvious examples are the destruction of peoples and cultures through colonization and genocide, or attempted genocide.

We can, however, learn from the Passion of Jesus and from the past, and we can attempt to undo some of the damage inherent in, and flowing from, the evils of the past

The great need is for us to listen to the prophets of the present. While the crowds follow their leaders or act out of acceptable beliefs of the time, the prophets see at present what the crowd will see only in the future. We need the prophets and we need to listen to the prophets. Remember, prophets are in danger simply because they are prophets. They offer unpopular solutions to our problems. They are killed or silenced in some way by the established powers who will suffer some loss of power, money or possessions if the voice of the prophet is heeded.

We wonder how Christian people missed the evil in things we now see as obviously evil. Some of these are not in the distant past, but whatever age they were in, they were wrong: systematic genocide, torture, trading in human beings are examples. There are things happening now that could cause future Christians to wonder at our lack of Christianity. Among these are our miserly foreign aid contribution, our fear of losing anything through generosity to the underprivileged, selfishness in the consumption of resources, our attitude to the plight of millions of refugees and racism among Christian people and communities. The

*Prophets see at present what the crowd will see only in the future ... We wonder (now) what sort of love it was which would have us believe that eating a piece of meat on a Friday would result in the eternal loss of God?*

attitude of the Church to shared responsibility and consultation, the presumption in the Church of the Roman rite that the gifts of priesthood and celibacy are both required for a person to be ordained, the role of women in the life and ministry of the Church, the teaching of the Church on sexual matters, and the whole style of Church decision-making and government could be added to the list.

I believe that more suffering is caused by attitudes than is caused by what might be regarded and admitted as sin. Destructive attitudes, left unchallenged, gradually become accepted attitudes and acceptable attitudes in a community. Attitudes of belligerent confrontation as ways of solving problems, racial abuse and discrimination, incivility and the diminishing of social responsibility in the quest for self-satisfaction, are not only increasing, but seem to be developing as the accepted response to life.

In what way can members of the Church be more in touch with the reality and beauty of the Gospel and with the Spirit of Jesus, the prophet, to be able to see through the false promises of prosperity obtainable only by selfishness, and happiness offered for the price of the lives and happiness of others? What sort of Church would it take to make it possible for us to have the wisdom, knowledge, understanding, courage and love to be the voices that speak out and the hands that lift up the downtrodden?

It is easy to criticize the Church of the past and even to laugh at things that were matters of serious consideration and the cause of much distress. We wonder what sort of love it was that would keep a religious sister from the funeral of a parent or that would have us believe that eating a piece of meat on a Friday would result in the eternal loss of God. What we must do now is to look at the present, and to discern with the mind of faith and love what things are conducive to the life of the Spirit in us as individuals and in our life as the people of God.

# 6. Longing for the "impossible"

When we long for a fuller expression of the life and service of Christ in his Church, that is, in the baptized, we are longing for something beyond mere human effort. We are hoping for something beyond human nature. Our belief is, however, that the baptized possess a gift beyond human nature. It is this gift—grace, the life of God within us—that we must allow to flow through us. The sacraments and the way they are administered and lived, preaching and pastoral work, are the instruments of this life of God within his people, and the instruments of helping us to know and accept the wonder of God within and to live this wonder.

There are good people of every religious conviction, and good people who have no religious convictions or even reject all religions. Christians are called to move to a goodness reflecting the all-embracing goodness of God, whose life they share in a special way.

Three things in our moral code reflect this and call on this power. The essence of the Christian life is supernatural union with God through Christ. To be true to this reality, Christians call on this indwelling power to live the way Christ lived, each in his or her unique way.

The three things I refer to are universal love, total forgiveness of all, and true humility. It is natural to love those who appeal to us or those who are generous to us, but to love everyone is more than natural. It is possible to forgive and to manage with people who have offended or harmed us, but to forgive one who, to take an extreme example, kills a loved and innocent child, is beyond human nature. We don't even know what this forgiveness requires or how it should be felt or expressed. Humility is a much misunderstood virtue and is very often misrepresented or caricatured. The truly humble person has a deep self-knowledge, a true self-acceptance and acceptance of others. Comparisons are not important, rivalry is not part of life and competition is reserved for fun and games. The humble person will have much more chance of universal love and total forgiveness because the humble person leaves to God the things that are God's.

To judge, convict and condemn are possible in relation to offences against the civil law because we have the facts of what the law states and the facts of the conduct of the accused. Comparing the two, a judgment is possible. We have no facts to guide our judgment with regard to the state of human beings in their relations with God. The prayer of Jesus from the cross contains these elements. He asks forgiveness for those who mock and torture him. Then he makes the observation, "they do not know what they are doing" (Lk. 23:34). Then he commits all to God, saying, "Father into your hands I commit my spirit."

If we have not reached this sublime state of being and living, that is not surprising. What is necessary is that we long for it and strive for it and respond as best we can as we are called upon to love with generosity and to be open to a process of forgiveness when forgiveness is difficult. We do not have to test ourselves with hypothetical cases. We love and forgive real people and in concrete circumstances. The beginning of the process is to admit our need for help. We need the grace of God if we are to act in a way which reflects the sublime goodness of Jesus. We need the means that Jesus has provided to help us: his sacraments and his wisdom, life and presence in human beings.

*When forgiveness has been given and accepted, the power of sin is broken; its force for destruction no longer exists.*

Jesus gave extreme examples to teach us that the impossible is possible with God. "Yes, it is easier for a camel to pass through the eye of a needle than for a rich man to enter the kingdom of God." "In that case," said the listeners, "who can be saved?" "Things that are impossible for men", he replied, "are possible to God." The strange picture of a mulberry tree flying through the air and being planted in the sea was painted by the words of Jesus immediately after teachings on the very things we have been considering. At the end of chapter 16, St Luke gives us the story of the rich man who ignored the poor man, Lazarus, and suffered the consequences of his own self-love and discrimination. Christian love does not discriminate against those who are outsiders: "and at his gate there lay a poor man."

The disciples are challenged further when, at the beginning of chapter 17, St Luke gives the teaching of Jesus on forgiveness: "If your brother does something wrong, reprove him and, if he is sorry, forgive him. And if he wrongs you seven times a day and seven times comes back to you and says, 'I am sorry,' you must forgive him." The reply of the apostles is an admission of the impossibility of it all. "The apostles said to the Lord, 'Increase our faith'." It was then that Jesus told them of the power which can make the impossible possible. The Lord replied, "Were your faith the size of a mustard seed, you could say to this mulberry tree, 'Be uprooted and planted in the sea,' and it would obey you" (Lk. 17: 6).

The power of hatred and revenge is immense. They destroy life and happiness in individuals and, when incited, are the instruments of destruction and misery of millions. They are reinforced by fear, lies, racism, and even religion. The vicious cycle of revenge can be broken only by the healing power of humility, which will lead to dialogue, an attempt to understand others and their needs, and the hope of forgiveness, and even the opening for love. When Jesus said, "Receive the Holy Spirit. For those whose sins you forgive, they are forgiven; for those whose sins you retain, they are retained" (Jn. 20:22-23), he was not going back on what he had already said about there being no limit to forgiveness. What he was saying implied more than a sacramental power to forgive sins, entrusted to the apostles and their successors. There is a profound reality embedded in this saying. He is calling his followers to be forgiving people. The vicious cycle of revenge and non-forgiveness will always be retained until forgiveness breaks that cycle. His followers are to be the ones to lead the way in breaking the cycle of revenge, hatred of others and hatred of self, perpetuated by unforgiving hearts.

When forgiveness has been given and accepted, the power of sin is broken; its force for destruction no longer exists. When sin is retained, forgiveness rejected and refused, the evil power is retained. We are all called to be the ones to set about dissipating the power of evil contained in what is, to a large extent, an unforgiving world.

# 7. No First- or Second-Class Christians

I have offered an interpretation of: "Receive the Holy Spirit. For those whose sins you forgive, they are forgiven; for those whose sins you retain, they are retained" (Jn. 20:22-23), which carries the responsibility of forgiveness and the breaking of the cycle of evil to the whole people of God. This is not to deny the reality or the value of a sacrament for the forgiveness of sins, but to bring the necessity of forgiveness into perspective as an essential element of the everyday life of every committed Christian. I take the point made in St Ephraim's Commentary on the Diatessaron: "Lord, who can grasp the wealth of just one of your words? What we understand is much less than what we leave behind, like thirsty people who drink from a fountain. For your word, Lord, has many shades of meaning, just as those who study it have many different points of view. The Lord has clothed his word with many hues so that each person who studies it can see in it what he loves. He has hidden many treasures in his word so that each of us is enriched as we meditate on it."

In popular preaching and interpretation, I believe we have impoverished the life of the Church by applying many passages of the Scripture in a narrow way as though they were addressed to clergy and religious. The call of the rich young man is not only a call to be a priest or a religious. It is the call to all to "come follow me" (Lk. 18:23) as Jesus invites us to leave behind all that impoverishes our spirits. The dialogue of Jesus with Martha and Mary (Lk. 10:40ff) is a call to all of us to be aware of the presence of the Lord. It is not a condemnation of industrious people

*There are no divisions in the Gospel calling — as if lay people were called to obey the commandments and those specially chosen were called to live by the precepts of perfection.*

nor an invitation into a convent. The beatitudes are addressed to all followers of Jesus.

There are no first-class Christians and second-class Christians separated by classifications of lay, religious and clergy, as though one class had to become more Christ-like. There are no divisions in the Gospel calling — as if lay people were called to obey the commandments and those specially chosen were called to live by the precepts of perfection. In fact, there are only two basic commandments: the commandments to love. These apply to all and will be lived out in the keeping of all other commandments and precepts.

Miracles can happen and will happen when we allow God to love us and allow his love to work its wonders through us. Jesus promised such a miracle. It was not anything to do with changing the course of nature to prove his presence. It would, however, work through human nature when human beings made way for the power of God in their lives and in their communities. This is the miracle which will convince the unbelieving. These are the words of Jesus, "Father, may they be one in us, as you are in me and I am in you." The next words tell of the outcome of this startling unity in love: "So that the world may believe it was you who sent me" (Jn. 17:21). These words have been commonly used in reference to divisions among different Christian churches. They are spoken to the disciples and they are about every one of our communities, small and large.

Jesus assures us that people would be startled into admiration, which would lead to belief, if they experienced a community of believers in that loving unity which is the reflection of the unity of the Trinity. Such a community would really bring about the presence of God with power.

# 8. The Fear Has Gone—And So Have They

If the teachings of Jesus are to go out to all nations and to people of all times without change, this could happen only by and through his sustaining presence. The doctrine of an infallible Church follows logically from the commission and command of Jesus to his disciples. Orthodoxy, however, implies more than adhering to theological concepts. The teaching of the Church gives us access to the great, unchanging truths regarding the being of God and his coming among us as a human being, his saving death and resurrection, his continuing presence in the sacraments and our eternal destiny with him.

About these essential teachings of the Church, there are not only the official declarations of the Church Councils, but a living Church—the people of God—loving and accepting these teachings across the ages. We see reflected here the Church's own teaching on Christ's abiding, infallible presence:

"The holy people of God share in Christ's prophetic office. The entire body of the faithful, anointed as they are by the Holy One, cannot err in matters of belief. They manifest this special property by means of the whole people's supernatural discernment in matters of faith when, from the bishops down to the last of the lay faithful, they show universal agreement in matters of faith and morals" (*Lumen Gentium*, para. 12). ("Down to the last of the lay faithful" is an unfortunate expression.)

Throughout the ages this astounding unity of faith has held the Church together as a worshipping community bound by a common faith. It is in matters of everyday life and everyday relationships that difficulties arise. In this area we seem to have lapsed from a united voice into two voices, one called "official teaching" or "the magisterium", and the other described as "dissenting voices". We all have a dissenting voice within us which calls us to having things our own way. It calls us away from Christian generosity and love, to selfishness and sin. I am not referring to this self-centredness but to the voice within that cannot sing in unison or in harmony with a voice that speaks from a position of authority and is neither understood by the head nor accepted by the heart. I have referred previously to a voice that spoke from authority and used the persuasive power of fear. In many cases, people seemed to respond, not from love, not from reason, but from fear. The fear has gone and so have they.

There is not only the fear which the Church has in

the past tried to instil to control dissent. There is also the fear seemingly present in Rome now which cannot listen openly to challenge, criticism or opposing views of loyal and devoted members of the Church. It seems that this closed fearful mentality is also a factor contributing to frustration and the rejection of the Church by many as being irrelevant and out of touch.

There seems to be no attempt at all to tap the wisdom, knowledge and holiness of the whole body of Christ in a search for orthodoxy in teaching and clarity in communication in regard to human living and relating. It is no wonder that the faithful walk away and that the young mostly find no satisfaction or answer to life in a Church which seems again to have closed its doors and windows to the world. In general, where is there any message of joy or hope or even support for the adolescent struggling with changing relationships, facing the workplace, experiencing sexuality, accepting some responsibility in society?

*There is a fear seemingly present in Rome now which cannot listen openly to challenge, criticism or opposing views of loyal and devoted members of the Church.*

If we could trust the so-called ordinary magisterium of the Church, we would have more confidence in following it without the necessity of an order to obey. This ordinary magisterium, however, does not possess a great record for reliability when it enters into matters of natural or human science. Its teachings on marriage and sexual ethics have been abysmal. Any pastoral priest will know from experience the misery inflicted on people through commonly accepted teachings, now no longer held. The physical interpretation of the functions and purpose of God-given nature is, and was, a force for misery and destruction of the human spirit that needs healing and redeeming. Even today we could ask in relation to this body-centred moral theology, what is more important to take seriously: the coming into being of a new human life, or the physical means by which we prevent this life? What is more important in the physical and sexual expression of love: its depth of reality, or the time of the month in which it is most unlikely to conceive a child? What is more important: love and spirit, or caution and physical methods?

Our moral decisions should concentrate on the existence of life and on its quality.

A moral theology whose basis is mere physical function means very little and achieves very little in a world already so directed towards materialism. We are the very people who believe in an immortal soul, but seem to be so obsessed with bodily functions. How can we have a more spiritual Church, a Church which on every level is doing the things Jesus was sent to do? Let us look at each of those reasons for which he was sent and try to respond.

# 9. TRUSTING THE HOLY SPIRIT

If we are the Church which Jesus intended, we will be living with his Spirit and doing the things he was sent to do: the things he sent us to do. "As the Father sent me, so am I sending you" (Jn. 20:21) are the words Jesus says to his followers of all times. Jesus tells us why he was sent and thus why we are sent: "The spirit of the Lord has been given to me, for he has anointed me. He has sent me to bring good news to the poor, to proclaim liberty to captives and to the blind new sight, to set the downtrodden free, to proclaim the Lord's year of favour." This is the measure of our orthodoxy and authenticity as Christian communities of any size and at any level.

Take these ideas one by one. Jesus spoke and lived from the spirit of God who was one with him. This Spirit was his gift to his Church. It is a free gift, but can be rejected or stifled. It is significant that the Apostles and disciples reacted in two classic ways when danger was present. They dispersed and ran away, then after receiving the message of the resurrection they gathered, but then locked themselves away. The full gift of the Spirit at Pentecost gave them courage both to be free together and to go out into the wider world.

Two human psychological complaints which inhibit free action are claustrophobia and agoraphobia. Spiritual claustrophobia and spiritual agoraphobia both inhibit the free flow of the Spirit which would call us into closeness and into going out into the market place. If we want to be a Church open to the Holy Spirit, one to whom the Spirit has been given, a people anointed, we might have to admit that we need liberating from these inhibiting conditions.

Try calling people into any small community to share the faith with intimacy and you will know what I mean. Those people who have been courageous enough to hand themselves over to the Spirit who speaks when people gather in faith will rejoice in their new freedom. But they seem to be small in number. What is equally distressing is that in places where small communities have gathered to share the message of the Gospel and apply it to their life situation, fear has imposed restrictions and caused caution. There seems to be an equal fear of the openness required to enter into honest dialogue in the market place, or even to open up honest dialogue among the faithful in many situations.

The Second Vatican Council was a bold attempt to overcome these spiritually inhibiting complaints in the Church. The documents of the Council and documents immediately after the Council gave great hope that we were going to take the risk of talking to each other and to the world at large with honesty, faith, trust and hope, in the expectation of overcoming some of the misunderstandings and barriers that are the cause of so much human suffering and the barriers to the clear understanding of the beautiful message of the Gospel. Such structures as the Synods of bishops,

*It is difficult to understand a spirituality that fears to trust the way given by the Holy Spirit through the instrumentality of an ecumenical council of the Church. How could believing people come to the conclusion that they had to fix it up before damage was done ...?*

pastoral councils on every level and open, free and trusting dialogue and consultation, were all firm hopes. The Spirit of the Lord had been offered to us again, but the spirit of caution and fear began to take its toll. Certain matters were taken out of the hands of the Church at large and reserved for decision after limited, if any, consultation.

Before the Synods of bishops, people were offered the possibility of making a contribution. I remember how they gathered with an enthusiasm which was soon dissipated when documents emerged which changed nothing and meant nothing to those trying to live a loving Christian life in a selfish world. In the same way in many places people lost interest in pastoral councils at parish and diocesan level. Now there are decisions coming from Roman Congregations as though there were no Church at all throughout the world. If the Spirit that Jesus gives is to be received, it can happen only through living the gifts of the Spirit. Courage is the gift that will make it possible for the other gifts to be exercised in the whole Church for the good of the whole Church and for the good of all people.

As individuals and as communities and as a Church, we need to take the words of Jesus to heart and to apply them to the choice of living in the spirit or living in fear. "For anyone who wants to save his life will lose it; but anyone who loses his life for my sake and for the sake of the gospel, will save it" (Mk. 8:35). The fear of losing something by being open or by honestly seeking the truth will inevitably result in the loss of the life that Jesus wants us to have. Life has to change and grow if it is to remain life. Conserving what we have is important, but what we have is best conserved if it is living, in light and fresh air, not in darkness and stale inflexibility.

If we trust in the Holy Spirit and accept the outcome, eventually God will see us through. The way to the truth may be through the cross, but there is nothing unchristian about that. It is difficult to understand a spirituality that fears to trust the way given by the Holy Spirit through the instrumentality of an ecumenical council of the Church. How could believing people come to the conclusion that they had to fix it up before damage was done to the

Church? Yet this seems to have happened after the Second Vatican Council. The Spirit of the Lord has been given to us. Is it possible for us to accept the gift of life with gratitude, even though doing so may seem like losing our security and life as we know it?

# 10. Rebirth of the Child

The good news is the revelation of the extraordinary potential of human nature. In Christ, human nature has come to its ultimate potential. The good news for all human beings is that we are invited to this sublime state. Human nature and the Divine Nature have been united in human flesh. The Word of God, who exists in eternity, became a human being and calls us into a union with himself through which the Divine Life will be one with our human life. The natural place of the Word of God is with God forever. Since Jesus was human, he had to die. That is the end of all human beings as far as earthly life is concerned. Since this human being who died was God, this human being had to rise to be with God forever. Our natural end is death, but if the divine Spirit of Jesus is united to our spirit and lives in our being, then the outcome of our death will also be eternal life with God. The good news invites us to accept this totally free gift of God made through his Word. The death and resurrection of Jesus are the saving events into which all are invited.

We can do nothing to earn this supernatural gift offered to all, but Jesus tells us how to make a place for his Spirit. It is the calling of all those who are filled with this Spirit to be what Jesus was, but in our own way and in our own place and time. He not only preached the good news, he was good news. To be an effective preacher of the good news we, his Church, must also not only preach the words, but live the words. The significance of the Word becoming flesh did not cease with the resurrection of Jesus. Human life is the way God chose to bring human beings into his life. This has not changed.

The very first Christian message that St Paul received was that the Christ, who had become flesh, remained in the flesh and blood and in the minds and spirits of those united to him by faith. No wonder his writings keep reminding us that

*Heaven is not the result of the credit balance of a profit-and-loss account. It is the outcome, continuation and perfection of a relationship which already exists.*

the Church is the body of Christ and that Christ is risen. The impact of the encounter with the risen Christ on the road to Damascus was there to stay. "Suddenly, while he was travelling to Damascus and just before he reached the city, there came a light from heaven all round him. He fell to the ground,

and then he heard a voice saying, 'Saul, Saul, why
are you persecuting me?' 'Who are you, Lord?' he
asked, and the voice answered, 'I am Jesus, and you are
persecuting me. Get up and go into the city, and you
will be told what you have to do'" (Acts 9:3-7). Jesus
was living; he was the voice from heaven; he was the
voice on earth who would tell Saul what to do.

St John Chrysostom observed that the New Law
was promulgated at the descent of the Holy Spirit
from heaven on the day of Pentecost, and that the
Apostles did not come down from the mountain carrying, like Moses, tablets of stone in their hands, but
they came down carrying the Holy Spirit in their
hearts, having become by his grace a living law, a
living book. Jesus told us how to become this living
book. The way to living his life to the full and allowing
him to live in us and speak through us was simply to be
what God had made. We were to look at Jesus and see
the image of the Father. We, too, are the image and likeness of God. Our loving response to God's gifts of life
and grace is simply to live lovingly and gratefully
with, and through, what he has given.

Some of the things that Jesus said can be applied in
different ways or they can mean different things for
different people. The rich young man was asked to
leave *everything* and to follow Jesus (Lk. 18:23). Zac-
chaeus promised to give *half* of his property to the
poor and to pay back four times the amount he had
cheated from people (Lk. 19:8). Martha, Mary and
Lazarus *kept* their home and gave hospitality to Jesus
(Lk. 10:38-42). Taking a saying of Jesus on its own,

and interpreting it out of the context of the whole Gospel, is not the way to truth. There is, however, one saying of Jesus which seems to be imperative and which fits in with the whole context of the Gospel. I think it will tell us how to be the living word of Jesus. We will examine its implications.

"Let the little children come to me; do not stop them; for it is to such as these that the kingdom of God belongs. I tell you solemnly, anyone who does not welcome the kingdom of God like a little child, will never enter it" (Mk. 10:14-15). This is the statement of Jesus which tells us of the way to the kingdom. The journey with and through him is one which takes us back to what God intended us to be. Thus it takes us forward to life to the full as God intended us to live and enjoy it.

The story of the Garden of Eden has the profound message that will be our starting point. Like many other parts of sacred scripture, this story has lost its impact because we have missed the message through looking at details and matters that concern sciences rather than the spirit. This is a story of the destruction of the child. Its destructive attitudes are passed on from generation to generation. An original sin created an accepted way of responding to life, which is destructive to life. The story tells us about those things common to life. God created us for happiness and endowed us with all we needed to be happy. Someone comes along and tells us that we need more, that we should have more, that we should be better than we are and that these things are there for the taking. We are unhappy with being what we are, and so enter into the process of becoming someone else. From facing each other and the world openly and with nothing to be ashamed about, we find that we must cover ourselves and be ashamed of the person God has made. There is great significance in the fact that the characters in the story, having attempted to go beyond their capacity, feel the need to hide and to cover up. The child was dead, but could come to life again. Jesus is the way, the truth, and the life restored.

If we, as individuals, and as a Church, are to enter fully into the Kingdom of Heaven, we must firstly recognize and accept the need for this new way which is freedom through truth and full life through freedom.

The child we seek is the child who is loved and loving, expresses beliefs and feelings, expresses those things without shame or fear of being wrong, admits ignorance, asks questions, admits fear, expresses wonder, asks for help, is spontaneous, lives in the present and has hope in the future.

The experience of life, ours and the lives of others, will instruct us as to how the child has been suppressed. The lessons passed on because of the original sin, are messages of caution, the need to prove one's worth, comparison and competition inculcating shame and envy. People have heard: "Don't make a mistake, don't make a fool of yourself, don't speak out against the majority, don't talk about religion or politics, don't show how you feel, you are expected to do as well as your brother and sister, you must come first, don't show up the family." Then there are the messages that destroy true and genuine self-esteem: "You are bad, wicked, useless, not worth talking to, wasting all the effort and money spent on your education. It is important to accumulate wealth, to be secure through power and to get the better of other people."

Destruction of people through the sins of cultures and families and through each other, has changed loving, playful, creative children into self-centred, self-protective competitors. The result is the inability to communicate with openness, respect and love in the search for truth. It is little wonder that relationships on the personal level, community level and international level, are so often more destructive than creative.

Redemption of this destructive evil and the rebirth of the child that Jesus spoke of, cannot come through the automatic effects of any sacrament. The power of the sacraments will come into action through the way God planned: through human nature. The incarnation is basic to redemption.

Becoming the little child is the way to the kingdom because it is the acceptance and acknowledgment of God's creation of me. It allows the kingdom to enter my life and being. The poor are the only ones to whom the good news means something simply because they are not self-sufficient. They admit their need and have not usurped the power of God by taking from his children what is theirs by right of birth.

The kingdom is a relationship with God that implies a relationship with the children of God. This is so here and in the perfect kingdom to come. Heaven is not the result of the credit balance of a profit-and-loss account. It is the outcome, continuation and perfection of a relationship which already exists. This relationship of love is the initiative of God himself. We are invited to allow him to love us and to love through us. We allow his love to work the impossible in us so that it radiates from within us and out to all of his creatures. We become one with the One who is loving creator. All sin is destructive simply because it is contrary to what we are: the image of the loving creator.

# 11. LIBERATED LIBERATORS

It follows from what has been observed about the good news that its effect will be to liberate captives. Jesus was sent to bring liberty to captives and new sight to the blind. We are that presence of the liberating Jesus. Just as the bearer of the good news must be good news, so too the liberator must be liberated to be a true liberating force.

If we are to be liberated from the things that enslave us, we must firstly acknowledge the presence of those things, accept that they are there and confront them with the truth of the Gospel. This we must do with the enslaving forces within ourselves. Mostly we can do this only with the help of others. Have I the courage to look at the truth of what motivates me, what inhibits the freedom of my responses, what I am afraid of, and what gives me satisfaction, pleasure and joy? The call to receive the kingdom as little children is a call to live in the present, accepting all its reality. That reality consists of what the past has made us, what the present gives us, and that there is a future for which we prepare and determine to some degree.

These things apply also to the community of the Church at all levels. Let us try to respond to reality. We must accept the sorrow of loss, the mistakes of the past and the missed opportunities that have in some way contributed to the present situation. Confirming past mistakes to prove we were not mistaken is no way forward. Just as an individual person needs to talk about the things inside so that they will be seen in their true perspective, so honest dialogue is necessary in the community of the Church. To exclude faithful people because they might ask the wrong questions—or come up with solutions that will disturb the present power structures—is not the response of Christians striving for the truth in childlike trust.

We have the example of the response of Jesus to both ecstatic joy and terrifying fear. Read Lk. 9:28-36. He tells of the transfiguration of Jesus. Notice how Jesus stays with the experience. He listens to the voice and then moves from the experience to enter into its implications. He is fully with the reality on the mountain, and fully with the reality of having to come down from the mountain. The disciples almost retreat into sleep. It seems that while they saw his glory, they missed the message of "his passing which he was to accomplish in Jerusalem". Having received only part of the message, they responded in a different way from the response of Jesus. He moved on to respond to the whole of the reality. They responded as though the kingdom had come. The glory was there, it was good to be there, so let us do what people always do in holy places: put up some shrines. It seems that the reason they were to keep quiet about the event until after the resurrection was that Jesus did not want half-truths to be preached about him. The shrine that Jesus would offer to the Father was not to be one built by human hands.

Another example from the gospels of Jesus staying with reality and with his feelings is given in Mk. 14:32-42. Here Jesus is in agony in the garden of Gethsemane. He faces the reality of his situation, his mission and the inevitable outcome of living and stating the truth. He does not shrink from coming face to face with the truth and with the feelings he is experiencing. He does not deny that he needs the comfort and support of friends and he does not shrink from going to them to ask for support. This is *Our calling is to set captives free. Have we made more captives than we have liberated?* true Christian life taught by the Word of God in action and in his passion. The disciples take one of the classical means of escape and denial. The situation is too much to face so they sleep. Sleep, work, play, food, drink, flight and drugs are part of normal life, health and growth, but as means of escape they can turn us from living a full life and facing the truth into frightened people living in the shadows. When the inevitable happened, Jesus faced it with courage and calm, having already faced and accepted his feelings and his commitment. The apostles, having gone through a process of denial, fled in the face of danger. "And they all deserted him and ran away" (Mk. 14:50).

As people who are called to set captives free, we have to work continually at being free ourselves. Nothing that is true can ever really make us captives. Facing the truth of who we are may be uncomfortable, but in the end it will be liberating. In helping others to be free, we are called to be fully present to, and for, the other. Individuals and communities seeking freedom and truth are in desperate need of those who can be so totally themselves that they pose no threat to others becoming their true selves.

How do leaders in the Church see themselves? Are they called to be the people in perfect control of themselves, with no doubts or fears, or people in search of the truth along with all other human beings? In the human situation, the solution to problems and the answer to questions are most likely to come, not from an authority that has all the answers, but from the search of patient, listening people speaking from facts, beliefs, experience and feelings enlightened by the Gospel and trusting in the abiding Spirit of God. Here there is no preconceived outcome that must be the end result after a pretended consultation. The outcome is open. It may be a convenient, comfortable one or it may be inconvenient and difficult to accept and implement. These things matter, but the only determining factor is the honest attempt to arrive at the truth.

An example of this type of dialogue is given by St John in the story of the encounter of Jesus with the Samaritan woman at the well in Sychar. Jesus accepts the woman as she is. He is not repulsed by the reality of this person so different from himself. His freedom, beliefs and integrity are in no way threatened by his openness to someone of different beliefs and way of life. He listens, responds with gentleness and interest until she feels free in his presence. His freedom has begun to liberate her. Along the way she tries to take the discussion from the present confrontation with reality into a religious discussion. This is a common ploy for people who find the present agenda too close to the bone. Jesus deals with her question, but what is important here is not religion, but a human being—a child of God who is loved into recognizing someone reflecting divine love.

Are we as Christians and as a Christian community involved more in holding onto religious beliefs, or more involved in liberating captives of religious beliefs, prejudices, racism, political systems, trade and financial structures, poverty and oppression of all kinds?

Our calling is to set captives free. Have we made more captives than we have liberated?

If we really trust in the power of Jesus the healer, we need not be shy about saying we are sent to bring new sight to the blind. First of all, our mission is to help people see life and relationships in a new

light and with new vision. Difference is often seen
and used to promote rivalry. This rivalry is both a
source of power for those in control and a source of
wealth to those who can manipulate it. It results in wars
of different kinds. We have wars of words, wars of
division and hatred, trade wars and wars that involve
fighting, maiming and killing. Some suffer, some
make a profit out of all of these. Jesus came to make
things better, but are they any better after all of these
years of christianity?

We are supposed to be the instruments of giving to
the human family the new vision that we are all
God's children and thus we are brothers and sisters.
Millions of Christians are in this world community.
What sort of a Church do we have then?

Secondly, the power to give the blind new sight is
not restricted to this spiritual insight and vision,
although this will determine the generous love and
the will to give physical sight to thousands. The
vision of thousands depends on the availability to
them of a simple eye operation to remove cataracts. We
can supply the money and the skills necessary to
accomplish this if we want to.

# 12. STANDING WITH THE DOWNTRODDEN

We have been examining the statement of Jesus as to why he was sent, and therefore why we are sent by him. We have come to "He has sent me to set the downtrodden free." This freedom for the downtrodden is our business as followers of Christ who came to liberate the oppressed.

We could ask very pertinent questions in this regard. Where are the downtrodden on my agenda and on our agendas as Christian communities? Do we recognize their existence or deny they are there? Who are they in our own community and in our own land? Who are they in the world? Do they have a place in my prayers and hopes, in my political thinking, intervention and voting? Do they appear on the agenda of the parish pastoral council, the diocesan pastoral council, the council of priests, the bishops' conference or the synods of bishops? If they do, do we address their concerns with the energy and resources with which we address matters concerning the smooth functioning of our own lives and communities? Are the stated concerns of Jesus at the top of the agenda, or something we have to pay attention to out of a sense of guilt, or because some prophetic person is making an issue of the matter and creating a nuisance?

The purpose of good law is freedom. Its spirit, its words and its enforcement, when necessary, enable people to interact with that balance of self expression and freedom which also gives respect to these human qualities in others. Where there is a lack of respect of the rights of others, laws will multiply. Since it is the vocation of Christians to set captives and the downtrodden free, we have a special role in society. It is not only laws that dictate the attitudes and responses of society. Custom and accepted attitudes hold powerful sway in determining the way minority groups and the less powerful are regarded and treated. Attitudes towards children, the aged and minorities are a measure of the culture of any society. Crimes against the least powerful in a society with a highly developed culture will be viewed as the most terrible of crimes. However, the collective conscience of any people can be dulled or even manipulated by the constant repetition of messages from authority figures. Among these are political leaders, religious leaders, the mass media, pressure groups and peer groups.

Individual Christians, and Christians as the people of God, are called to go deeper than law or custom or accepted cultural responses to the downtrodden and the less powerful members of society. It is to these poor that the Gospel is preached with meaning. They, according to Jesus, are the ones who will understand. So it is not only that established members of the community should come to the poor and the down-trodden to give them all they need, but they come to learn, to interact

*That there are very few "different" people in our Church communities must tell us something. It would be Christian if the differences were there but were welcomed rather than viewed as disruptive.*

and to share life. In the Church there are not the givers and the receivers, but people acting with respect for each other, learning from each other, giving to each other and receiving from each other.

For full life it is important to give with love and generosity; but it is also important to receive graciously and with gratitude. The Church should never be seen or preached about only as the Church for the poor. It will reach its destiny by becoming the Church of the poor.

It is a real concern when people express the feeling that they are not good enough to join with a Christian community, or that they are not presentable enough, or not the type of person who would be made welcome. This feeling can come from a misunderstanding of the loving quality of the community in question, or it could come from the experiences the person has had previously. That there are very few "different" people in our Church communities must tell us something. It would be Christian if the differences were there but were welcomed rather than viewed as disruptive.

Open dialogue with the disillusioned and the alienated would be a powerful teacher if we had the courage to undertake it in the spirit with which Jesus spoke and listened to the woman at the well at Sychar (Jn. 4:5-24).

Our calling to bring freedom to the downtrodden will mean that we stand with them, and thus suffer with them. The downtrodden of the world are almost inevitably the indigenous peoples, alienated through the imposition of laws and cultures that have no meaning to life and give no respect to these people as possessing a developed culture with its own laws and presumptions. The downtrodden of the world have been and still are so often those who are, or whose ancestors have been, treated as the goods of others. Slavery and its results still bring disgrace to God's creation. Standing with the downtrodden will cause suffering because the raising up of downtrodden people will call on the proud and the rich not only to change their attitudes, but also to risk their wealth. Change in the political and social structures will be an advantage to the poor, while the rich will see it as a threat. Patient, constant effort, backed by the power of the Gospel and the mutual support of Christ-like people, has achieved wonders and can continue to achieve wonders.

The Church has been a great and effective liberator in setting people free from the oppression of communism. Being an atheistic system by its own definition, it was obviously contrary to all that was sacred to the Church. Its system was, of course, contrary to the spirit of freedom contained in the Gospel. It is true, however, that other systems with similar or worse implications for the freedom and dignity of human beings existed and even still exist The wholehearted attack on communism was, and is, justified because of its view of humanity. I wonder, however, if the fear of "the left" has not caused as much damage as the system itself. Over-reaction and exaggerated fear of anything which resembled this system has itself caused immense suffering and allowed, and even supported oppressive systems because they were opposed to what was seen to be coming from the left.

Thoughtful response is always a more valid human attitude than reaction from fear. This fearful reaction to so much of the past has left us with a legacy of divisions which we are still trying to overcome by making the Christian response we should have made in the beginning. I think of the reactions to scientists, the theologians of the Reformation, scripture scholars, and courageous bishops and priests who at present are trying to bring some hope of liberty for captives.

When Jesus touched the lepers, allowed himself to be touched by the "sinful woman", took meals with tax collectors, and had dealings with gentiles and those outside the establishment, he was not looking at theological cases, but at God's beloved children. For the scribes and Pharisees, the woman caught committing adultery was a theological case. They asked Jesus to solve a problem in law. Their theological discussion could blow away with the dust he wrote in. For Jesus, she was not a case to be discussed, but a child of God who needed to be lifted from the dust, forgiven and loved. Then she was free to go, to live true love and true freedom.

# 13. Laws Don't Change People

Jesus is the good news to human beings. There is nothing in the Gospels to indicate that he came to redeem only part of us. God's human creation is the whole person: body, feelings, mind and soul. This is what he created, and loves. Human beings are created in the likeness of their creator who is absolute goodness, love and happiness. What we have been considering in the proclamation of Jesus regarding his coming among us, has given attention to the human needs that rely on our loving and just relationships with each other. Our happiness will depend on the freedom which God gave us being exercised and being allowed to be exercised. For this we have basic human requirements, the absence of which will limit life in some way.

Jesus goes on to tell us that, having liberated us from the injustice that can deny our God-given rights to life and freedom, he is the year of God's favour. He, and therefore his followers, are God's instruments for forgiveness, amnesty and reconciliation with God and with each other. He comes to proclaim communion with God in the most sublime way that is possible. He is the gift of the holy year which abolishes all barriers to God. This is more than any other holy year. He is the eternal year of God's favour. He is the holy gate through which we go into the holy city, into the very presence of the Holy One.

In preparation for the coming of the Lord's year of favor, John the Baptist told us of the need for making room for him in our hearts. "Even now the axe is laid to the roots of the trees, so that any tree which fails to produce good fruit will be cut down and thrown on the fire" (Mt. 3:10). Is this the good news of the Lord? If we wonder, we may reflect that it is very good news to know that change is possible and that there is one who can give us the strength and the power to change, and can endow us with a gift whose power for change we could never imagine. John goes on: "I baptize you with water for repentance, but the one who follows me is more powerful than I am, and I am not fit to carry his sandals; he will baptize you with the Holy Spirit and fire" (Mt. 3:11). The call will be impossible to answer without the fire of courage and love that the Holy Spirit will give to those who allow him to give it to them.

It is a miserable state to try to live the life of a follower of Jesus without this holy fire of inner conviction and love. Many personalities have been stunted and twisted from trying to live in conformity with laws without love. The end result has often been a stoic life of self-protection, superficial relationships and conformity through fear. We have also experienced a legalistic and stilted response to the later calls for conversion and reform made by the Second Vatican Council, and by subsequent reforms flowing from its spirit. It is not possible to graft the Spirit onto a living person or a living community. What Jesus had to give had to be received into fresh and open minds and spirits. His gift is not an outside addition, but a union of spirits. The incarnation is the model of the Church. We are the body of Christ in which human nature and divine nature live with the same life spirit.

In responding to the decrees of the Vatican Council and to subsequent documents, what many seem to have attempted is to keep a spirit of law and preach a spirit of greater freedom. People whose practices were determined by law from outside had no reference point when they were offered general guidelines of freedom of conscience in making decisions about matters for which previously they were given detailed directions. For others, if the law was not there or was indefinite, the obligation did not exist. Jesus meant his followers to be wiser, deeper and more loving than this. He said, "For I tell you, if your virtue goes no deeper than that of the scribes and Pharisees,

*Many personalities have been stunted and twisted from trying to live in conformity with laws without love.*

you will never get into the kingdom of heaven" (Mt. 5:20). The kingdom is within and its nature will shine out in the actions which come from its life-source. He told his followers that the fruit produced by the tree will depend on the nature of the tree.

A saying of Jesus most appropriate for any attempt at reform or change that will produce real and lasting good, refers to this very choice between inner reform and the mere patching up of what we have, preserving it in case we lose something. It is precisely through this mentality of fear that the greatest loss is sustained. In the words of Jesus: "No one puts a piece of unshrunken cloth onto an old cloak, because the patch pulls away from the cloak and the tear gets worse. Nor do people put new wine into old wineskins; if they do, the skins burst, the wine runs out and the skins are lost. No; they put new wine into fresh skins and both are preserved" (Mt. 9:16-17). Reading this, I cannot help thinking of the people of the Church being torn between con- flicting authorities, communities splitting apart and parents wondering what their children were being taught in Catholic schools, children not responding to what was previously held to be most important, and parents and pastors lamenting their departure from the worshipping community.

It seems that we were passing on a teaching learned through catechetics and practiced as part of our culture, or even through fear. There are—and always were—outstanding exceptions who have internalized the message and live out of a true faith and union with God. For these, change meant a call to greater holiness and a response to God and to the good of others which needed no law and very few guidelines to direct its outcome.

There seemed to be a presumption that priests and religious needed constant nourishment for the interior life and that the laity needed no more than the commandments and the laws of the Church to be preached and interpreted for them. We have divided God's people into the privileged class and the less privileged.

Whether priests and religious took advantage of their privileged position in this regard is another matter. The important matter is the presumption that the large majority of God's holy people were, and are, incapable of very much depth of spiritual life. It disturbs me when I hear of people, young and not so young, discovering meditation and going off to some other religion to learn how to profit from its practice. They are completely ignorant of the Catholic tradition and the many schools of spiritual life coming through that tradition.

I remember, years ago, at a time when the senior priest was absent from the parish and I had the responsibility of spiritual director of the women's sodality. I spoke to them about meditation and gave them some idea of a method of undertaking this way of prayer. When my colleague returned, he rebuked me for presuming to speak to "his ladies" about meditation. He was a good and admirable man. Did his attitude, however, reflect a widely held belief that we could not risk trusting the laity with too much freedom, even in prayer?

I believe that one of our great needs is to internalize the beautiful message of the Gospel. Gospel reflection, meditation and contemplation should be part of the normal life of a Christian. The message, and living the message, are both too beautiful and too difficult to leave to chance or the vague hope that something may rub off.

One of the difficulties of living the Gospel is accepting with real conviction the fact that God dwells within me. Since this indwelling is true, the eternal year of favor, which Jesus came to proclaim and to bring about, has already begun. As we live and deepen this reality, the relationship grows between God and us. The eternal reality—heaven—will be the continuation and the outcome of this relationship. This is an essential part of the message proclaimed by Jesus and passed on to his followers to possess and to proclaim.

When the people observed that Jesus spoke with authority, they were not referring to the authority which came from anywhere or anyone outside himself. The authority was his total integrity. He was what he said, and he lived what he was. The Father and he were one, and when people saw him, they saw the Father. In our prayer of meditation or contemplation, we seek this unity with God. The Church is the community of people impelled by this Spirit of love, truth and unity.

# 14. HOLY GIFTS TO EACH OTHER

For the gospel to touch our hearts, penetrate our minds, move us to a deep, loving relationship with God and arouse our sense of social justice, we need time and quiet to allow the mind of Jesus to penetrate our minds. Without a close relationship with Jesus, we could remain Christians on a superficial level. The Christian life is at the same time interior and exterior. Those people who deny any need for externals in their spiritual life—people who say, "I talk to God and find him in the beauty of nature, and I have no need to belong to a Church"—have missed the point of Christianity. Jesus called us into a relationship of love with God which implied a relationship of love, care and concern for God's children. There is no such thing as a Christian without involvement. It is impossible to be human without relationships, and Christianity is supposed to make a difference to these natural relationships.

Our whole life and our relationships are the way to God because they are his gifts.

The existence of the sacraments is testimony to the fact that it is through spirit and matter that we receive God's free gift of his own life-grace, the gift of God's Spirit. If we are to use the extraordinary gifts of the sacraments in a way which helps us to accept God's life to our fullest capacity, then we must take full advantage of all they have to offer in their ritual and in their depths of meaning for life.

God has chosen to come to us through each other. The most wonderful and significant of those others is Jesus Christ, the Son of God himself. In his life he used ordinary things to teach, to heal and to be the instruments of his life and abiding presence. Physical proximity to Jesus did not necessarily achieve anything by way of a change of heart. Jesus was close in place and physical relationship with people, but could do little to move their hearts because of their lack of faith. St Mark records that "he went to his home town" and then, after his encounter with the people of that place, we read, "And Jesus said to them, 'A prophet is only despised in his own country, among his own relations and in his own house'; and he could work no miracles there, though he cured a few sick people by laying his hands on them. He was amazed at their lack of faith" (Mk. 6:4-6).

The sacraments are visible signs of an unseen reality, but their effect depends on faith. The deeper the faith, the more powerful will be the outcome of the fruits of that faith. In the signs are the rich messages of what they promise in this life and in eternity. The signs and the words are not chosen lightly. Nothing lives without water; bread and wine sustain life; oil is a sign of giftedness and of healing; the imposition of hands is a sign of election and the giving of office; the words of human commitment and of forgiveness are a sign of realities that exist before words are spoken. All of these things have a communal dimension and are not merely personal favours. Thus it is impossible to draw their maximum richness without the involvement of a believing community.

The Rite of Christian Initiation of Adults is an excellent example of making full use of the sacramental rites. In this process there is acknowledgment of all things human and divine necessary to undertake the journey of faith and to come to its end, with human nature prepared to be immersed into Divine nature. It is not only a process of learning certain truths which are to be accepted; it is a process of coming into contact with Christ in his believ-

*It is impossible to be human without relationships, and Christianity is supposed to make a difference to these natural relationships.*

ing people. God is present in all things and in all people. When faith is brought to bear on these, a change takes place. Within the believing community and with the power of Christ's abiding presence, ordinary things become extraordinary. The people searching for God bring their own questions, doubts and beliefs, while the faithful bring their faith, hope and

love. Their gifts of wisdom, knowledge and understanding are revealed as they share their own struggle
and human weakness. Human interaction, discussion, instruction, hospitality, care and concern, are
all part of a process of God's gifts coming through
the reality of his Church in this place and time.

It is interesting to notice how Jesus speaks to the
crowd and, when they have dispersed, a few remain to
get closer to the heart of things. After Jesus spoke
about the bread of life, St John records: "After this,
many of his disciples left him and stopped going with
him. Then Jesus said to the Twelve, 'What about
you, do you want to go away too?' Simon Peter
answered, 'Lord, whom shall we go to? You have the
message of eternal life, and we believe; we know that
you are the Holy One of God'" (Jn. 6:67-69). These
were the few who, in the end, gathered around the table
at the Last Supper to learn the meaning of this real
bread from heaven. After the parable of the sower
(Mk. 4:1-9) St Mark writes: "When he was alone,
the Twelve, together with others who formed his
company, asked what the parable meant" (Mk.
4:10). These are not isolated cases. It seems that
there is something special about sharing the faith in
small groups. The Gospel message is not merely
something to be learned, but something to be
chewed over, digested and absorbed into one's
being. Jesus is the bread of life in more ways than
one. Whichever way we receive him, we should not
rush the meal.

# 15. Don't Be Afraid to Come Close

The last point brings to mind the Holy Eucharist. Jesus gave us a visible, audible and communal way of remembering him and his message, and of being in touch with his own presence. He extends his real presence across time and place to be the saving gift for all. The offering of our redeemer to the Father and our reception of him in the Eucharist are placed in the context of a holy meal and a remembrance ceremony. There are stories, exchange of gifts, speaking and listening, praising, asking, greetings and thanking. We speak to God, God speaks to us, we give to God, he gives to us. All the while, we interact with, and acknowledge, the presence of each other and the needs of the whole body of believers, and our brothers and sisters in the human race.

It is not easy to do all of this with the faith and human involvement that it deserves and requires in order to receive the maximum benefit from God's gift. Just as the Apostles and a small number of disciples acquired an intimate relationship with Jesus from being with him in a small group, it seems that we have a better opportunity to gain that intimate knowledge and love of the Lord when we gather in his name in a situation where we can listen and speak, express our needs, and ask the questions that we need to ask for our growth in faith and knowledge.

Those who have experienced the value of coming together with people of faith and love will realize the potential of a Church composed of communities such as these. I have been asked to spend the day with groups of people with different needs, who are seeking a deeper relationship with God and some understanding of how the realities of life—even those that are very destructive and hurtful—can be put into a context of meaning and fuller life. Such a group of people, seeking, hoping and believing, has great potential for good.

On some of these occasions we constructed the whole day around all that takes place within the Mass. We came together and after the greeting paused to reflect on the forgiving love of God, and prayed the penitential rite and the prayer of the Mass. The first lesson was read and each person went off with a copy of the reading to be alone and to reflect on it. After an hour's reflection we returned to share whatever we wanted to share with each other. There was no hurry; people paused to consider what had been said and, at times, made some response. When all were satisfied, we responded by praising God with the psalm. From there we went to share a simple lunch together. After lunch the Gospel was read. Again, we dispersed for reflection and, after an hour, we shared our thoughts and interacted. The prayer of the faithful was the outcome of our sharing. The eucharistic rite followed with a peaceful pause after Holy Communion. When Mass was over, we shared a cup of coffee while expressing mutual thanks for all that had happened.

Administering and receiving the sacraments in a way like this offers an example of the power of the word and the sacraments when they are given time and space in an atmosphere of faith and mutual care. The feedback from these experiences has been extraordinary.

*Those who have experienced the value of coming together with people of faith and love will realize the potential of a Church composed of communities such as these.*

People have come through almost impossible barriers to forgiveness and acceptance of the reality in which and with which they live. The Church becomes present with the presence of Christ in all his forms. He is obviously present in this community gathered in his name: that is, in his spirit of love. He is present in the scriptures read and received in faith, in the praying community, and in the Eucharist

We, the Church, need to tap the rich gifts that we have from God through Jesus. The Church has developed a teaching and a ritual with all that we need. This teaching and this ritual, however, seem irrelevant to many and distant to others. To tap these treasures we need a way to make them both relevant and close to life. When Jesus spoke of faith, he seemed to speak more of an ability of his followers to trust him than of an adherence to a set of beliefs. Beliefs are vital to the conduct of life, but do not always determine that conduct, as we all know too well. Trusting God with the outcome after following his ways is the sign of the faith that Jesus longed for in his disciples.

We have examples of this in the Gospels. When Peter walked towards Jesus on the water, then began to sink, the faith that Jesus asked of him was nothing to do with a set of beliefs to which he gave assent, but everything to do with believing and trusting that Jesus could sustain him. The same is true of the faith referred to by Jesus after his call to forgive over and over again: the faith that can transplant the tree from where it is to the middle of the sea. This faith can come only by seeking and finding, knocking and having the door opened by Jesus. Desire will lead to search and the search will be with Jesus, present in all his forms among us. In fact, when we accept him in the poor, in the community, in his word and sacraments, we are finding him as we continue searching. He told us we would be surprised to know that he was in those who were hungry, sick and in prison.

Present structures seem inadequate to satisfy this need for intimate communion with Christ present among us. I will look at alternatives later.

# 16. Courage to Look in the Mirror

It is impossible to know, and of no use to know, whether this age is better or worse morally than any previous time. We do know that our crimes are more widely publicized and the harm we do to each other is on a larger scale. The thing that does not seem to have changed is the way we have of justifying our actions. We have always been good at believing that God is on our side. Now, people are more likely to use terms such as "my freedom, my rights and justice" as the god which justifies their actions. It has always been difficult for us to admit that, in satisfying the voice of my god, I may be destroying the freedom, happiness, or even the life of others. The Pharisees, Pilate and the others who justified their actions in getting rid of Jesus, the enemy of religion and the state, acted no differently from people of every age. Jesus continues to be crucified by self-centredness. St Luke's Pharisee continues to make the observation that he is not like the rest of humankind (Lk. 18:11).

To combat this inclination towards denial of reality and denial of guilt and responsibility, we have the gift of the sacrament of reconciliation. Here again is a way to personal self-knowledge and to social responsibility. The sins we commit never remain only with ourselves. They have an effect on others. Thus the Church has always seen the necessity of personal confession of guilt and communal reconciliation. Again, it is only through a realistic and human use of this sacrament that our human needs can be addressed.

The Church has developed means of our coming to terms with the human reality of ourselves and the community in which we live and make our way to God. The particular examination of conscience, the chapter of faults, the sacrament of reconciliation are all very healthy combinations of the flesh and the spirit in the context of community. Many people will not have heard of the chapter of faults or the particular examination of conscience. These are examples of those things offered to the few who were deemed to be called to a holier life. Again, unfortunately, these gifts of the accumulated wisdom of the ages, instead of being offered to all, have been rejected and discarded on a large scale even by those who knew of them, because of misuse and misunderstanding of what we had.

The particular examination of conscience was offered to me in my younger days as a way of looking at faults, and, month by month, rejecting one after another until I was perfect! It *could* be a way of taking time to reflect on the day in an attempt to see what was significant, what I might have missed as a way to greater love and service, and an attempt to see what God was saying to me through the people and events of the day.

I have never personally experienced a chapter of faults so I must speak from second-hand knowledge. If it was, as I have been told, an exercise in thinking up some things to say or of being accused and humiliated in front of a community, it had lost its great potential for being a way to community listening, speaking, understanding, searching for peace and unity, healing and forgiveness. There is something very healthy and very Christian about a group of people coming together and speaking from the truth of what they feel, perceive and believe their actions and words conveyed, and of saying what their perception of the actions and words of others was. So much hurt is sustained because of misunderstanding.

*We have always been good at believing that God is on our side. Now, people are more likely to use terms such as "my freedom, my rights and justice" as the god which justifies their actions.*

The way towards understanding is through dialogue in a non-judgmental, peaceful and trusting atmosphere. Such a gathering would presume that all would speak the truth and accept the words of the others as what they believed to be true. The group would agree that all could speak their minds with the presumption that what was being said was out of love and never designed to hurt. It is this truth that will set us free. This gathering in love and in an attempt to accept, understand and forgive is not restricted to those who live in religious community, but is the means to the fullness of life we all seek through interacting with each other. Thus interpreted and used, the chapter of faults was a way to self-discovery and the understanding of others. Thus it was a way to God.

The sacrament of reconciliation is designed to help us admit our guilt and accept responsibility for our actions. Having done this with repentance, we are reconciled to God and to the community which we have offended. The Church brought to our attention the need for a more realistic use of this sacrament. In recent times we have been reminded that mere recitation of sinful actions may never get to the basis of why we do these things. The renewal of the rite gave attention to the two basic realities involved: our attitudes to life and the communal aspect of sin. The Church offered three options in the liturgy of the rite. The first option of the rite drew attention to our attitudes to life, and the other two options drew attention to the communal aspect of sin.

Unfortunately, it seemed to be another case of trying to pour new wine into old wineskins. Individual confession is most valuable as a way of coming to a deeper realization of self and of the results of one's attitudes. It is not about merely changing the design of confessional boxes, or about reading a piece of scripture before one rattles off a few sins. It seems that an honest attempt to offer people the opportunity of taking advantage of this wonderful sacrament would imply individual appointments. Offering only a half hour before Mass is inviting people to go back to the quick-recitation-of-sins mode.

There are those who would appreciate the healing touch of Christ through the body of his Church, who may have a lot to say, but are not ready or able because of their own personality to come face to face. Perhaps this will happen later as confidence grows. For these people, the Church designed the third option of the rite of reconciliation. It is part of the Church's ritual and sacramental structure, and thus an instrument of grace. It offers us a means of knowing and experiencing the forgiving Lord alive in his Church and in the actual community in which we live. Here we admit we have hurt others, weakened the community and not allowed the grace of God to flow fully into us and through us. Individual confession does not take place. Absolution is pronounced over the group. It is so appropriate to our times and was the product of the wisdom instilled in the Church that discerned this. Yet the central authority in the Church has all but suppressed this option.

We should respond with gratitude to God and with trust in him and take what he has given us. What causes the caution? If it is fear, then love will cast out fear. Let us be a Church which is the model of love.

I do not question the value of individual confession. Bringing sins and the source of sin into the upper consciousness, and admitting our responsibility under the guidance of a caring person whose advice we respect, is surely a very valuable gift offered by the Church. Humility and wisdom are the gifts that both penitent and confessor will need to cultivate for the grace of God to work to fullest capacity. They are the gifts of the Spirit that we are assured of receiving when we ask with faith. If there is a gentler way of coming to the point where this form of reconciliation is effective, we should take this way.

It may be useful to remember that the decrees and laws emanating from the Council of Trent were made in a situation that was defensive and in a time of reaction to error and to abuse from within the Church and from outside. Reason and truth are not always best expressed in defensive and reactionary situations. One big difference between the Council of Trent and the Second Vatican Council was that the first was a defensive reaction and the second was a response to needs.

# 17. Sacrament of Holy Nakedness

The word and the spirit of Jesus are readily received by those who become like little children. The kingdom of heaven is theirs. Those who know and accept themselves, who accept others as brothers and sisters and not as rivals, who do not worry too much about tomorrow, are able to share what they have and be open to others, are free to become the good news of which Jesus spoke. All of the sacraments are designed to help us along this journey and are the earthly instruments of the life of heaven.

There is one sacrament particularly designed to help us find the lost or suppressed little child in us. The outward signs of this sacrament are not water, oil, bread and wine, or any other inanimate thing, but human beings, human love and human commitment. That sacrament is marriage.

One of the first messages we get about ourselves from the Bible is that we cannot reach our potential

alone. "It is not good for man to be alone" (Gen.
2:18), has profound meaning and must be taken seriously by those who seek union with God. We come to
God with, and through, each other. The riches contained
in this teaching of scripture have been untapped by
those who see marriage as something less than the
God-given means by which we reach our potential.

The needs each of us has for intimacy, trust, a
sense of being safe with another, and of love shared and
expressed in every way possible, are able to be ful-
filled in this holy sacrament. I have already referred to
the ways in which the child in us can be suppressed. If
the message has been one of covering up and of lack of
self esteem, then in the intimacy of trusting love in marriage, we have the opportunity of uncovering, and of
being and expressing ourselves. The message of the
Garden of Eden is a profound one. Total openness to
God and to the other, and total self-acceptance, are
expressed beautifully in the word picture of two
people walking naked together and before God,
delighting in his creation of themselves and of all
creation.

Then comes the invitation to be more than they
are, to be something else. It has been heard and,
unfortunately, accepted ever since. Be gods your-
selves, take control, don't let them pull the wool over
your eyes and make a fool of you. When the temptation
is heard and they respond by giving in to it, they can no
longer be happy and comfortable with reality. They
begin to live a lie, so it is necessary to cover up
because they are ashamed of the person whom God has

created. The story tells us that this is exactly the result of their living the lie. They hide and they cover up. Redemption from this falsehood is possible. We can again become whole by being ourselves.

The sacrament of marriage implies the coming together of two people who love and trust each other so much that there needs to be no pretence. In this intimate community of people, each can be perfectly comfortable in living the total truth that makes that person who he or she is. I remember preparing to go on a weekend sharing session with a group with whom I was doing a course in counselling. We were not long on the course and this was new ground for some. One of the group, a person with a very responsible position at work and well established at home, expressed a feeling of uncertainty and insecurity about the venture. His problem was that he knew exactly who he was at work. He was in charge. He knew what his role at home was, but who was he in this new situation where there was no definite agenda and no given roles?

*If one partner betrays the love and trust of the other and walks away, surely the sacrament has dissolved, just as the presence of Jesus is no longer in the dissolved host when it becomes something else.*

So often we act out our roles and fit into the mould formed by the social environment in which we live without coming to terms with the unique reality that is self.

Being safe and comfortable with another person who loves us for who we are is the very climate we need for full growth in freedom and the happiness that comes from self-acceptance. Marriage is the sacrament of holy nakedness: the place and situation where one has no need for pretense or cover-up. This should be what we are always but, unfortunately, we fall far short of this way of living. Having experienced the delight of the freedom of being oneself with one person, we may have the confidence to go further in letting the truth set us free.

The frequent caricature of marriage is of people losing their individuality and freedom and submitting to the ball and chain. The objective of the sacrament of marriage is just the opposite. It is in the trusting and intimate relationship of marriage that a person should be able to find the true self and develop interaction in a climate of truth, so as to develop a state of freedom never possessed before.

All of this may sound too idealistic, but Christianity is a high ideal offering us a way of life we can live only by the grace of God. To be able to receive these gifts, however, we must first know that they exist and that they are possible. Then we must learn how to be open to what God offers us through other people. It is important to let people know what is possible through entering into a fully loving and trusting relationship. It is important to teach the knowledge and skills necessary for good and open communication.

We have been taught that marriage is one, excluding other such relationships, that it is permanent and that it is for the procreation of children. An essential quality, whether children are possible or not, is the procreation of each other, the co-operation with the creator in his will that each of us reaches our potential.

Regarding the dissolution of marriage, we have to look at what makes marriage. Taking an analogy from the other sacraments that can be received more than once, we observe that when the sense-perceptible elements of those sacraments are no longer present, then Christ is no longer present in that particular way. The Holy Eucharist is an obvious example. Since love and commitment for life are the basis of the sacrament of marriage, when they no longer exist, is it not reasonable to conclude that the sacrament no longer exists? If one partner betrays the love and trust of the other and walks away, surely the sacrament has dissolved, just as the presence of Jesus is no longer in the dissolved host when it becomes something else. The sacraments are for holiness. They were made for us, not we for them.

The teaching of the Church forbidding sexual intercourse before marriage is founded on the teaching that this physical expression of love is so complete that it expresses outwardly the most profound human commitment and love. To act with integrity, the love and commitment represented and expressed by sexual intercourse must first exist. Then, a ritual expressing this commitment must take place because of the social implications of the commitment. The most important social implication is, of course, the coming into existence of children from the union. The permanency of marriage is not only with reference to the stability, security and worth of the two people, but also for the security, stability of life and love of the children. This mutual love and its sexual expression must exclude others, is permanent and is conducive not only to the begetting of children, but to their happiness and development into mature adults.

We know that people fail in these high ideals. Many in the world today do not give sexual intercourse this profound significance. Very often people have an inaccurate perception of the person they marry, or they fail to cope with changes that inevitably take place in themselves and in their partner. They may even enter into a marriage with the objective of changing their spouse to suit themselves. Inadequate preparation and inadequate knowledge of what marriage is for are not uncommon. It seems also, that, from time to time, married couples would gain a great deal in mutual understanding and in personal growth if they took time to look deeply at their relationship and to renegotiate things that were taken for granted or not fully understood.

If, for any reason, the attitudes that the Church says are necessary to make intercourse legitimate no longer exist, how can it be moral for legally married people without these attitudes to act them out physically, while single people are forbidden to cohabit? If the teaching on the significance of sexual intercourse is true, would it not be moral to help such people to separate, rather than forbidding them from separating?

For the sake of children they may choose to make a sacrifice and merely stay together. The children may
profit from this unselfish act if their parents can live
together in mutual respect and peace. Otherwise,
one wonders if children could profit from a situation of
constant tension.

The one thing by which to judge whether our
choices are for sin or for grace is love, for God is
love, and grace is the life of God within us. "Those who
do not love me do not keep my words" (Jn. 14:23-24).
"This is my commandment: love one another as I
have loved you" (Jn. 15:12). These are the sayings of
Jesus setting the standards for the basis of all moral
theology and all Christian law.

With regard to the law, Jesus did not observe
any law which contradicted love. The Pharisees and
lawyers spoke of cases in law, but Jesus responded in
terms of persons, loved by God and deserving of the
respect which that love implied. Instances are the
woman caught committing adultery, Jesus healing on
the sabbath, the disciples picking and crushing corn on
the sabbath and Jesus breaking the law to touch
lepers.

In a personal, intimate Church, we can have the
same attitude. We would not be dealing with cases, but
with friends whose qualities we would know. As
those in the community speak to people and know
them, they are no longer cases to which unchange-
able principles are applied as though no person
existed, but they are human beings with responsibilities
to each other and to the community.

Take the case of a family in such a loving and caring community. The family members love each other and are generous and caring people who accept their family and social responsibilities. They seek the grace of community strength and the grace Jesus offers in the Eucharist. One partner in the marriage has been married previously and his former wife has remarried. He accepts the fact that his former marriage was a real marriage, but also recognizes the fact that the former marriage no longer exists. Those things which made the sacrament no longer exist. It would seem sinful to have continued in the union and to act out a lie.

These people are presented with the reality of their situation and can be offered some options. To respond to the call of Christ, they must choose whichever of these options is the most loving, the one that will open the way to the life of grace. The "official" options seem to be: that the man return to his first wife; that he leave his present wife, make a decision about the children and live as a single man; or that he stay where he is but not act as a husband—living as a single man with a single woman in the same house and family.

Which of these choices is realistic: a choice which reflects the real situation, is life-giving, conducive to a healthy, moral and happy life? Which is caring for all the people concerned, loving for all, and, therefore, conducive to the life of grace? None of them, it would seem.

It would not only be impossible to return to the

former spouse, but it would be wrong. Jesus assures us that we cannot love God and treat other people as though they were mere objects to be disposed of. It would be an act of injustice for this man to walk out on a wife and children who love him and depend on him as he depends on them for a full life, love and happiness. To stay where he is and act as though he had no sexual feelings for the one he loves, and to demand that she should act in this way, is quite unrealistic and even conducive to the destructive forces of sin in the breaking up of something good and loving and in the working out of frustrations in other ways. Now then, it is never possible to say that I have no option but sin. We can never be in an impossible situation with God. The choice that the loving community, through its representatives in this pastoral situation, will help this family to make will be the one that is the most loving. Grace is found in facing the situation and making the decision.

Somewhat similar to the situation of these people is the situation of a priest who has found that he does not have the gift of celibacy and has married. Under the present discipline of the Church, he is no longer acceptable as an approved minister to the community acting on behalf of the Church. But since his present situation is the reality, there seems no point in making him and his spouse feel as though they are outcasts. The most loving, therefore the moral response, would seem to be to accept the reality and to welcome these children of God into the community with love and appreciation of any contribution they can make. Perhaps there will come a time when such a priest will be able to exercise his priesthood in the way he is able and willing to exercise this gift of God.

The Church we long for is a Church which facilitates the flow of goodness and grace in every possible way. Fear of the consequences of mercy, forgiveness and generosity cannot be from the Holy Spirit. "What the Spirit brings is very different: love, joy, peace, patience, kindness, trustfulness, gentleness and self-control. There can be no law against things like that, of course. You cannot belong to Christ Jesus unless you crucify all self-indulgent passion and desires. Since the Spirit is our life, let us be directed by the Spirit. We must stop being conceited, provocative and envious" (Gal. 5:21-26).

It is obvious that to marry or not to marry are both human rights and human freedoms. What then of the self-development of those who, for any reason, are not married? Since we were not meant to be alone and cannot reach our potential in isolation, then intimacy of some kind is necessary for all. All of the things I have said about a secure relationship in which to trust and grow are necessary for all human beings. That we do not take the gifts that God offers us in marriage or in the community is obvious from the many inadequacies displayed in human nature: the inability to relate with truth and openness, the fear of generosity, fear of and discrimination against those who are different, misuse of power, sexual instinct and physical strength, crimes against children and

the poor. We need others and intimate, trusting relationships with others, to help us grow and to accept and
love the person God created when he made us.

All of this has something to do with the sort of
Church we have and the Church we can hope for.
The Church is the body of Christ, the instrument of
God's gifts and wisdom. But the Church is this
group of human beings who can be an open channel of
grace or, in many ways in its members, a barrier to
God's love and life. Which we choose depends on
us.

# 18. "You Are the Church," But—

The faithful have heard for years that they are the Church. When they have shown concern about the way the Church is going they are told, "You are the Church." I watched a programme on television which was an attempt to listen to the concerns of faithful Catholics. The matter of priests who had married and were therefore no longer acceptable as ministers in any way in the liturgy, came up in the discussion. There were others who had married and had waited for a dispensation without a positive response. A questioner asked the bishop on the panel where the compassion of the Church was. His reply was the Church showed constant compassion in its care for the sick, the poor and the afflicted. It was the answer these people had heard time and time again. They are the Church. They are the healing hands and the consoling words of Jesus.

Their level of frustration only rose to further heights and it was expressed in frank words.

Yes, they are the Church when it comes to being the ministers of compassion, the people who give to the poor, visit the sick and those in prison, and comfort the dying. These pastors and faithful lay people are the hands of the healing Jesus. But when it comes to their being part of the body of Christ in making the decisions which determine the way the Church is governed and the rules determining the discipline of the Church, they are outsiders.

Since the Church is a human reality, it needs structures. A body needs a frame as well as a heart and mind. The heart and the mind are the essential gifts for all times and places. The message of Christ is the same yesterday, today and always. The framework and the language through which the message is delivered are like any body and any language. They change constantly. If the body does not change, it dies.

What is useful in one place or in one age may mean very little to another, or may be destructive to another. It is regarding these changeables in expression, in discipline and in structure that we need the wisdom and experience of the whole body of the faithful. A Church which gave credit to its members for having intelligence, wisdom, true concern for good, and a knowledge of its teachings as well as of the conditions in which they live and work and in which those teachings are applied—such a Church would be a real sign of the presence of Christ in all of his members. It would be a wonderful act of faith in what we believe: Christ is in his Church, wherever that Church is.

This faith is very poorly expressed when there are a lack of trust in the local Church and an excessive centralization of decision-making in matters not essential to the faith. When matters of discipline are given the importance that matters of faith should have, it is a sign of that caution which seems to say that it is too risky to trust the outcome to the people of God and the Holy Spirit who dwells in those gathered together in one faith, one baptism and one Lord.

The official teachers in matters of faith have come together in Sacred Councils over the ages, to define and express the content of faith in terms and in language applicable to their times, and to address matters of importance for their times. The last of those gatherings, the Second Vatican Council, spoke to its times and to the problems and people of those times. It was the great pastoral council, not called to condemn any specific heresy, but to respond to the needs of the Church and the world in a positive way. The council called for the very things we see now as being so vital in bringing the Church to its potential.

Less centralization, more genuine consultation on every level, speaking to each other with frankness and confidence, and co-responsibility, were all seen as ways forward. The lay faithful were given credit for having special skills and knowledge that would be brought to bear on pastoral concerns, while their clerical leaders were asked to listen, discuss, decide together with the laity, and to bring their collective wisdom to bear on the administration of the spiritual wealth of the Church. The separation of clergy and laity should never have reached the level at which it was, and the Second Vatican Council decreed that this separation should be reformed to bring the Church closer to being the People of God—the

*Less centralization, more genuine consultation on every level, speaking to each other with frankness and confidence, and co-responsibility, were all seen (by Vatican II) as ways forward.*

Body of Christ and God's Faithful People—as it is meant to be.

These teachings about the way the structure of the Church should be reformed came from the highest teaching body in the Church: an Ecumenical Council, called by the Pope, the decrees of which were accepted by the fathers of the Council and approved by the Pope. It is distressing for faithful Catholics to reflect how far we have fallen below the high ideals proposed and spelled out with such clarity and with the obvious authority of the Holy Spirit.

# 19. A Priesthood without Clericalism

The sacrament which has the most profound effect on the constitution, the function, and the effectiveness of the Church, is the sacrament of Holy Orders. All Christ's faithful people are baptized into Christ—priest, prophet and king—but the ordained Christian receives these gifts in a way that enables him to act in the person of Christ in a specific and necessary way to make the sacrament of the Holy Eucharist possible. It is for this reason and for the passing on of this gift that the Sacrament of Holy Orders is so vital in the life of the Church. Christians may meet to pray, be of mutual help and support to each other, and to be a force for social justice; but an element essential to the full meaning, strength and life of the Christian community is the Eucharist.

In places where there has been a dramatic fall in those seeking to serve their fellow Christians as priests, we have been looking at ways to function as the

Church without the service of the full time, resident priests we have been accustomed to. The priest I learned to be was one who was celibate, lived in a presbytery with at least one other priest, was available at any time of the day or night—except for one day which was spent in recreation with other priests and family. This priest was minister of the sacraments and preacher, but also adviser and guide in all manner of life situations. He would eventually become financial and business manager of the temporal goods of the Church.

We have discovered that there are other ways of doing things, and people other than the priest who can do them better. In the best of parishes, responsibilities have been shared and consultation is seen as vital to decision-making. This does not solve the problem of the declining number of priests nor does it address the fact that the priest is mostly on his own now in the presbytery, the only full-time person on the job at all times, the one who is most readily available in any emergency, the one confronted with everything from tragedy to trivia.

It is possible to have an ordained ministry without the requirements the Church has attached to ordination. Two of the things that have inhibited the full life of all of the members of the Church as participants in Christ's ministry are the over-emphasis on the role of the ordained ministers, and their separate, very distinct lifestyle. The Church and, at times, society, made the separation very clear. In the Church there were clergy, religious and laity and the first, second and third estates in society. Special dress, lifestyle and laws, made it clear to the faithful that the position of the large body of Church members was at best second-rate. I do not believe that Jesus ever meant things to be this way.

There were certainly people called by Jesus, and appointed by the Church later, to accept special responsibilities, but all were called to serve with equal dignity and respect for each other. "You know that among the pagans their so-called rulers lord it over them, and their great men make their authority felt. This must not happen among you. No; anyone who wants to become great among you must be slave to all. For the Son of Man did not come to be served but to serve, and to give his life as a ransom for many" (Mk. 10:42-45). This is the charter that Jesus gave for service in is Church. It is not only about service, availability and hard work. It is about the whole style of authentic Christian leadership. "The slave to all" does not call the tune to which his master dances. The slave listens to the master, is careful to know the master's will and to satisfy the master's needs. The whole body of Christ, with all its members, is both master and servant at different times and in different ways.

It is clear also that there is no distinction in rank or in respect for any servant of the community. As ministries developed, it seemed to be necessary to make this clear to the Church. The body of Christ is not only part of the body, but the whole body with all its members and all their gifts. St Paul found it necessary to

remind the Corinthians: "Nor is the body to be iden-
tified with any one of its parts. If the foot were to
say, 'I am not a hand and so do not belong to the
body,' would that mean that it stopped being part of
the body? If the ear were to say, 'I am not an eye,
and so I do not belong to the body,' would that
mean that it was not part of the body? If your whole
body was just one eye, how would you hear anything?" (1Cor. 12:16-17). Then he continues:
"What is more, it is precisely the parts of the body that
seem to be the weakest which are the indispensable
ones" (1Cor. 12:22).

It is interesting to observe that when he names the
different gifts, he
does give them an *Marital state or gender*
order, the first being *seems to have nothing,*
apostles, but later, *essentially, to do with the*
coming as separate *matter of who is more*
gifts, are teachers, *capable of any service to the*
prophets and good *Church or of any position of*
leaders. "Now you *responsibility.*
together are Christ's
body, but each of you is a different part of it. In the
Church, God has given the first place to apostles, the
second to prophets, the third to teachers; after them,
miracles, and after them the gift of healing; helpers and
good leaders, those with many languages. Are all of
them apostles, or all of them prophets, or all of them
teachers? Do they all have the gift of miracles, or all of
them teachers? Do all speak strange languages, and all
interpret them?" (1Cor. 12, 27-30).

How did we ever conclude that all of these gifts should or could be contained in the one human being? That we did seem to come to this conclusion and to work from it has been to the suppression of the many and varied gifts that God invested in the whole body of his Church.

Perhaps it is the very next verse of this letter to the Corinthians that can bring about the change necessary for us to have a Church alive with the gifts of its many members: verse 31 of chapter 12: "Be ambitious for the higher gifts. And I am going to show you a way that is better than any of them." Then chapter 13 begins with St Paul's eulogy to love: "If I have all the eloquence of men or of angels, but speak without love, I am simply a gong booming or a cymbal clashing" are the opening words to a piece of scripture which is the key to Christian service and Christian law-making for service.

No ministry is given as a personal privilege to the recipient. Each is called, not to be served, but to serve. It seems reasonable, therefore, that the requirements for accepting a ministry and for being accepted by the community, should be the requirements best suited to facilitate the service to be given. There is nothing intrinsic to the ministry of priest that requires one to be celibate or a full time person financially supported by the community.

Firm faith, a good moral life, a sense of responsibility to the local Church and the universal Church, a love of prayer, a knowledge of the liturgy, a sensitivity to others, an ability to communicate and a reliable, stable personality would be some qualities necessary for the ordained minister who would preside over the community gathered to offer the Holy Eucharist. Other ministries would have their special requirements. The preachers, teachers and catechists would need a more thorough knowledge of sacred scripture and theology. Counsellors and people preparing their fellow Christians for the sacraments of marriage and reconciliation would require different qualities and skills.

We might solve many of our problems if we began to create small Christian communities whose members served each other in their day-to-day needs for worship, prayer, study, listening and counselling, care for the sick and needy, solace for the bereaved, and involvement in addressing matters of justice and charity for the local community, their country and the world. Many of the ways I have proposed for getting closer to each other and to God can be seen as possible only in small, caring communities. In such communities, every member would be striving to be full time Christian and part time minister. Every member would contribute in time, talents and finance. Every member or family would work to support themselves and to contribute to the financial needs of their worshipping community and of the wider Church, and to make some contribution to the needs of the poor.

Marital state or gender seems to have nothing, essentially, to do with the matter of who is more capable of any service to the Church or of any position of responsibility.

# 20. A Vision of the Church

The vision of the Church built up of small, caring communities does not in any way undermine the acceptance of the fact that, being Catholic, we are members of a universal Church and that the universal Church is made up of individual dioceses whose bishops are in communion with the bishop of Rome; it is he who presides over the whole Church as the point of unity in love and belief. He does this as servant of all.

In the above-mentioned vision, each diocese would be divided into smaller units than most present-day parishes. The determining factor would be the viability of the group and its capacity for the members to know each other and care for each other. The concept of personal salvation to the exclusion of the Church has been the factor which has weakened the Church as the sacrament of salvation for the world. We teach that Jesus founded a Church to be the instrument of his saving words and work. We preach that it is his will that all should come to him through the means he has made available, yet the faithful themselves have often acted and worshipped as though the Church were their own personal channel to be tapped into for personal grace and salvation. We have lived a contradiction to a large degree, by preaching the necessity of a community of believers while acting like a number of individuals doing the same thing at the same time and calling this a community. This does not, of course, apply to all, but religion as a private concern is very commonly accepted as part of the culture among Christian people.

The way to accept the Church that Jesus left us and that the Apostles founded is to become like that group of people who knew each other and cared about each other, and gathered to pray, share their goods and receive the Lord in the breaking of the bread.

To make this truly the Church, the bishop would approve these communities, accept their leaders and ordain their priests. All this would be done in consultation with the community. Leaders would emerge, candidates for ordination and the non-ordained ministries would present themselves for acceptance by the community and ordination or induction by the bishop. Some would need to undertake further studies, many of which could be part-time in the same way that many people already undertake part-time studies.

Members of the communities which make up

the diocese would be very much involved in the consultation process leading up to the choice of their bishop.

In this situation we would still need some people whose full-time duties were in service of the Church. The bishop, who has oversight of the whole diocese made up of these reformed parishes, would need to give his full attention to the pastoral care necessary to ensure the smooth running of the communities, their constant renewal, and their orthodoxy in teaching and practice. The Church would need its theological faculty where theologians were engaged in constant study and research, and were available to teach the disciplines necessary for the ministers to be able to offer a service worthy of ministers of the mysteries of Christ. The finance necessary to fund these works would come from the faithful as it does now. In fact, there should be much more money available for these necessities and for the poor if we create a structure less dependent on full time ministers and all that follows from this, and on large gatherings of people in little-used buildings.

Each minister would study those things necessary to have a sound knowledge of the Church and its teachings, but would specialize in those things necessary for the ministry involved. Thus the length and intensity of studies would not be as great as for one who was supposed to be available for every service in the Church's ministrations. Those going on to be full-time teachers would take on full-time studies. Each member of the community would provide his or her own living and accommodation. The Eucharist and the services offered by the group could take place in the homes of the faithful or in rented premises. The burden of purchasing, owning, maintaining, cleaning, repairing and insuring property would be a burden no longer carried by the faithful. With more personal and intimate knowledge of fellow members and of the community at large through

*We have lived a contradiction to a large degree, by preaching the necessity of a community of believers while acting like a number of individuals doing the same thing at the same time and calling this a community.*

those members, and with discussions on world needs, one would expect that the generosity of the people thus gathered would increase. There should be no shortage of resources to supply the necessary things to sustain the Church as a living, growing and caring body.

The modern means of communication, where they are available, make it reasonably easy for a group of caring people to be available twenty-four hours a day and seven days a week without any one person bearing too much of the burden. Such things as telephone systems, with an available parish number which can be transferred to as many places as are necessary, fax machines located in any number of homes, and computers containing all the information necessary make possible the task of distributing responsibility and providing constant care without the necessity of a central place or full-time employee.

Given a Church whose main thrust is the deepening of our spiritual life, pastoral care and missionary outreach, I believe we would have no shortage of priests or of ministers of any kind. The priest and the ministers in this parish community would be equal sharers in the ministry and mission of Christ. They would accept responsibility for the support of their own families and for their part as members of the body of Christ. None of what I have written is about the essential nature of priesthood, the theology of priesthood or those things specially reserved to the ministry of priests. It is about the clerical state, the image of exclusiveness that this term seems to imply, and about linking celibacy with the priesthood as though matrimony and holy orders were designed by Christ to be mutually exclusive.

If we are to go forward as the holy people of God, the Mystical Body of Christ and the Sacrament of salvation for the world, we must pay attention to the things essential to the faith and the teachings of Jesus and leave behind man-made structures and laws which have either outlived their purpose of being servants of the Gospel, or which in fact never really served the Gospel, but arose from an inadequate perspective of the beauty and dignity of what God has created and what Jesus renewed.

# 21. Ministries in This Church

The creation of a Church made up of small communities is not for the purpose of isolating people from the cares of the wider Church or the wider world. It is precisely for the opposite reason. Isolation from others is more likely to bring about isolation from the concerns of the Church and the world. People who listen, discuss, enquire and mix with others concerned for the good of all, will become involved in the decision-making and the activities necessary to bring about a more caring and just society. Thus these small Christian communities would come together in gatherings structured on something like a deanery and then in diocesan gatherings. For the considerations on how best to address a situation or a problem, they would send representatives. Liturgical celebrations could be organized in which the groups of the whole district would come together from time to time to gather around the bishop in offering the Eucharist.

On special occasions, the whole diocese would celebrate its unity and diversity when all would be invited to experience the reality of a Church of committed, caring and worshipping people gathered as one body, one spirit in Christ. The coming together of so many dedicated, informed and prayerful people, nourished by intimate association in prayer and service would really be a most powerful act of worship and confession of faith. It would be a body with a healthy head and a healthy heart.

Since the whole Church is responsible for its unity and its continuing outreach, the whole Church is responsible for supplying the resources necessary to make these things possible. Some full-time people would be essential for the facilitation and the administration necessary to make these meetings possible, for the co-ordination of the material coming in from the communities and for seeing to it that the decisions made by the bishop's advisory council, coming from the grassroots and taken by the bishop, were implemented.

This full-time commitment does not imply permanency in office, celibacy or priesthood. Whether in the small groups or in the diocese, ministry means service. When one can no longer serve with the full commitment, enthusiasm and energy required for the particular ministry, that person should be free to move on to something else. The Church keeps reminding its ministers that they are called to serve, not to be served.

Celibacy is a gift which many have received, and given so as to be fully available to the service of others. This is true not only of generous priests and religious, but of scientists, health-workers, scholars and teachers. At the same time, there are extraordinary examples of totally dedicated married people from all walks of life. There is no necessity to demand of any person the requirement of celibacy in order to prove that she or he is prepared to be totally dedicated to a calling.

The faithful with the gift of celibacy would, however, be ideal missionaries if they had that vocation. The Church cannot remain a Church which merely cultivates the life of grace in its present members and their children. It is by nature missionary. From the Church established in any place, there should come people who *When one can no longer serve with the full commitment, enthusiasm and energy required for a particular ministry, that person should be free to move on to something else.* are impelled by the Spirit to go out to others to preach the Gospel. The freedom from family commitments that goes with the gift of celibacy facilitates the free movement of the missionary. Such a person is free to give up home and stability, firstly to go off to learn those things necessary to preach the Gospel with meaning to those who listen in any place. These missionaries could be the people sent to establish the Christian communities of which I have spoken, both in their own diocese and in other places. What would make them different from missionaries of the past in many instances is that they would stay only as long as it takes to establish a community, then ask the bishop to hand the community over to the care of the local people, ordaining and inducting their chosen ministers.

Dedicated missionaries, being celibate, could either live in community or not; if not, they could go back to the community for rest and renewal between missions. Again, there seems no necessity to require a life-long commitment to a specific ministry. If one can no longer undertake a responsibility with conviction and with a whole-hearted dedication, we should not accept an empty attempt to go through the motions. A wholehearted, joyful service in another capacity is the response that seems to be authentic, healthy and productive of goodness for self and for others.

## 22. CELIBACY MUST BE TOTALLY OPTIONAL

I have mentioned celibacy as a gift to facilitate service to others. As a requirement made necessary for the receiving of other gifts, it seems to make no sense. In fact, to make it a requirement really weakens the force for good that it could have as a sign of goods other than those seen and felt.

We know from both Church teaching and Church practice that celibacy is not necessarily attached to priesthood. Since this is a fact, we could ask whether the requirement of celibacy from one called to be priest is an unjust demand.

The natural way of human development and apparently the God-given way to mature development for most people is through intimate relationships. The most common and the most natural of these is marriage. The first book of the Bible assures us that it is not good to be alone and that we need each other. One of the basic human rights that most people would admit to and accept without question is the right to marry. Christians would go further to say that barriers made by race, class or law of the land, which exclude some from the exercise of this freedom, are wrong. What God has given, we may not deny.

If God had denied marriage to those called to be priests, or had given every person called to the priesthood the gift of celibacy also, then there would be no question as to our wholehearted acceptance of these facts. But it is obvious from the teaching and practice of the Church that God did not make celibacy a requirement for priesthood. Married men are priests. It is obvious from human history, and from the observation of the existing situation, that not all those called to the priesthood have the gift of celibacy. To accuse all those good men who could not live the celibate life but knew they were called to the priesthood, and who loved that calling—to accuse them of some sort of perverse denial of a gift from God and a rejection of that gift would be both insulting and absurd.

No one is forced to become a priest. That is not the point. If marriage is a human right and a channel of grace from God and the priesthood is also a calling given to a person called to be married, is it not unjust to demand that that person must make the choice between two gifts from God, neither of which is exclusive of the other? The person called to be priest is being asked to reject a grace from God in order to follow the Lord. No wonder there is so much sadness in the lives of idealistic, unselfish men who either walk away from one love or another, or sometimes live a life of denial of their full humanity. I hope that those blessed with both the gift of *It is obvious from human history and from the observation of the existing situation that not all those called to the priesthood have the gift of celibacy.* priesthood and the gift of celibacy take the time to listen to those who are not thus blessed.

## 23. FOR THE PRESENT

There is urgent need for those who have the power to act to put the essentials of the faith and practice of the Church before non-essential, man-made, laws. That Church discipline, custom or law should be the obstacle to the spread of the Gospel and access to the Eucharist, or the other sacraments, seems a contradiction. The law exists to facilitate freedom and goodness, not to restrict them. The fact that certain laws exist gives them no special right to continue to exist. Their existence should be determined by the service they give to the Gospel of Jesus Christ. This calls for the humility needed to admit that change is necessary and that former ways approved and affirmed may not now be the best ways.

There are ways of discerning God's will and of seeking to know the way in which we should be proceeding. All we have to do is to let the Church speak. For Roman Congregations, or even a Pope, to

take matters affecting the life of the Church to themselves seems to be against the nature of the Church. It
has happened in the past, but is that authentic tradition? Or is it closer to the nature of the Church to see
any curia, either diocesan or universal, as the servant of
the teaching authority? The Pope is the one who
calls this authority together to preside in love and
seeks the truth in communion and service. Any ministry
and any gift from God to his people is not a personal
favor, but is given for the community and in service to
the whole Body of Christ.

What can we do while we are waiting for the
changes necessary to make the work and sacraments of
the Church more accessible and more appropriate in
their expression, to the people of our time? How can we
develop a living Church which will have some hope of
being all of those things which Jesus called it to be:
good news to the poor, liberty to captives, new sight to
the blind, the power to lift up the downtrodden and the
sign of the presence of God's favour?

It is not impossible to begin to create small communities of people who have these things at heart
and who would become more committed as they
grew closer to God through sharing his word and
love.

Starting from the present situation, when a
priest is no longer available for an existing parish or for
a new parish, we should not absorb the parish into an
existing one, nor hesitate to create a new one from one
too large. Perhaps the best way our most generous
and talented priests could exercise their ministry

would be as missionaries sent out to these non-priest areas to establish a community of faithful people who would bring the church into existence in their own parish. Most of the duties, as far as time is concerned, at present carried out by the priest, can in fact be performed by a deacon or a non-ordained person. These communities or parishes could come to a central place for the celebration of the Eucharist. Transport supplied by the community is not as great a financial burden as the building and upkeep of a church. Even if the number of priests were such that Mass became possible less than once a week, the gathering for prayer and the word would be the point of community strength and mutual support.

It would be the aim of the missionary priests to inculcate in the people an understanding of the Church which goes deeper than an obligation to law which would be inclined to say: "If no Mass is possible, there is no obligation." The ideal is, of course, that when a community of Catholic people gathers to worship on Sunday, they gather around the table of the Lord to offer his sacrifice and to receive him in the Eucharist.

The faithful throughout the world have been forced to accept less than Jesus promised. In this book suggestions have been made as to how we could make the Eucharist more accessible to the Church at large. No law should stand in the way of our access to this sublime gift.

Accepting and bringing about the necessary changes will be no simple task. It will entail conflict and struggle and involve loss of things familiar and treasured. But the real loss is in attempting to hold onto what we have because of nostalgia or the fear of change. Deep spiritual maturity is called for. We need to take Jesus at his word: "Anyone who tries to preserve his

*The fact that certain laws exist gives them no special right to continue to exist. Their existence should be determined by the service they give to the Gospel of Jesus Christ.*

life will lose it; and anyone who loses it will keep it safe" (Lk. 17: 33).

In many places in the world, if we hold off much longer from entrusting the treasures of the faith to the whole Body of Christ, we will have very few faithful to whom we are able to hand on any model of the Church. God will provide! God will provide in the way he chose to provide: through us, when we let him act through us.